ASPECTS OF LAW REFORM

The British justice system is an ancient one that has continually evolved to meet modern needs. In this set of three essays, originally presented as the Hamlyn Lectures in 2012, Jack Straw reviews some of the most important recent reforms to the system of British justice and suggests key areas in need of further reform. He focuses in particular on the criminal courts, human rights, judicial appointments and the relationship between the UK parliament, the domestic courts and the European Court of Human Rights. In all three cases, he argues that the British justice system is now in a healthier state than at any other point in his lifetime, but that there remains much room – and need – for improvement.

THE RT HON. JACK STRAW MP was the Lord High Chancellor of Great Britain and the Secretary of State for Justice from 2007 to 2010. He served as Home Secretary from 1997 to 2001, Foreign Secretary from 2001 to 2006 and Lord Privy Seal and Leader of the House of Commons from 2006 to 2007.

ASPECTS OF LAW REFORM

An Insider's Perspective

JACK STRAW

CAMBRIDGE
UNIVERSITY PRESS

CAMBRIDGE UNIVERSITY PRESS
Cambridge, New York, Melbourne, Madrid, Cape Town,
Singapore, São Paulo, Delhi, Mexico City

Cambridge University Press
The Edinburgh Building, Cambridge CB2 8RU, UK

Published in the United States of America by Cambridge University Press, New York

www.cambridge.org
Information on this title: www.cambridge.org/9781107043022

First published 2013

Printed and bound in the United Kingdom by Clays, St Ives, plc

A catalogue record for this publication is available from the British Library

Library of Congress Cataloguing in Publication data

Straw, Jack (John Whitacker Jack), 1946–
    Aspects of law reform : an insider's perspective / Jack Straw.
        pages   cm. – (The Hamlyn lectures)
    Includes bibliographical references and index.
    ISBN 978-1-107-04302-2 (Hardback : alk. paper) – ISBN 978-1-107-61816-9
(Paperback : alk. paper)
    1. Law reform–Great Britain.   2. Law reform.   I. Title.
KD654.S77 2013
340′.30941–dc23
                                                                    2013009482

ISBN 978-1-107-04302-2 Hardback
ISBN 978-1-107-61816-9 Paperback

CONTENTS

The Hamlyn Trust   *page* vi

The Hamlyn Lectures   ix

Preface   xiii

1 The future of the criminal courts   1

2 The Human Rights Act and Europe   25

3 Judicial appointments   51

Index   78

The Hamlyn Trust owes its existence today to the will of the late Miss Emma Warburton Hamlyn of Torquay, who died in 1941 at the age of eighty. She came of an old and well-known Devon family. Her father, William Bussell Hamlyn, practised in Torquay as a solicitor and JP for many years, and it seems likely that Miss Hamlyn founded the trust in his memory. Emma Hamlyn was a woman of strong character, intelligent and cultured, and well versed in literature, music and art, and she loved her country. She travelled extensively in Europe and Egypt, and apparently took considerable interest in the law and ethnology of the countries and cultures that she visited. An account of Miss Hamlyn by Professor Chantal Stebbings of the University of Exeter may be found, under the title 'The Hamlyn Legacy', in volume 42 of the published lectures.

Miss Hamlyn bequeathed the residue of her estate on trust in terms which it seems were her own. The wording was thought to be vague, and the will was taken to the Chancery Division of the High Court, which in November 1948 approved a Scheme for the administration of the trust. Paragraph 3 of the Scheme, which follows Miss Hamlyn's own wording, is as follows:

> The object of the charity is the furtherance by lectures or otherwise among the Common People of the United Kingdom of Great Britain and Northern Ireland of the

knowledge of the Comparative Jurisprudence and
Ethnology of the Chief European countries including the
United Kingdom, and the circumstances of the growth of
such jurisprudence to the Intent that the Common People
of the United Kingdom may realise the privileges which
in law and custom they enjoy in comparison with other
European Peoples and realising and appreciating such
privileges may recognise the responsibilities and
obligations attaching to them.

The Trustees are to include the Vice-Chancellor of the
University of Exeter, representatives of the Universities of
London, Leeds, Glasgow, Belfast, and Wales, and persons co-
opted. At present there are eight Trustees:

From the outset it was decided that the objects of the
Trust could be best achieved by means of an annual course of
public lectures of outstanding interest and quality by eminent
lecturers, and by their subsequent publication and distribution
to a wider audience. The first of the lectures were delivered by
the Rt Hon. Lord Justice Denning (as he then was) in 1949.

Since then there has been an unbroken series of annual Lectures published until 2005 by Sweet & Maxwell and from 2006 by Cambridge University Press. A complete list of the Lectures may be found on pages ix to xii. In 2005 the Trustees decided to supplement the lectures with an annual Hamlyn Seminar, normally held at the Institute of Advanced Legal Studies in the University of London, to mark the publication of the Lectures in printed book form. The Trustees have also, from time to time, provided financial support for a variety of projects which, in various ways, have disseminated knowledge or have promoted to a wider public understanding of the law.

This, the 64th series of lectures, was delivered by the Rt Hon. Jack Straw, MP. The first was held at the University of Leeds, his alma mater, on 6 November 2012 in the Moot Court Room of the new law building and chaired by Keir Starmer. The second was held on 13 November 2012 in the Alumni Auditorium of the University of Exeter and introduced by the Vice-Chancellor. The final lecture, chaired by Sir Stephen Sedley, was held at the Inner Temple Hall, London, on 4 December 2012. The Board of Trustees would like to record its appreciation to Jack Straw and to the two universities and their law schools, as well as the Inner Temple, who so generously hosted these Lectures.

AVROM SHERR
Chair of the Trustees
February 2013

1949   Freedom under the Law by the Rt Hon. Lord
        Denning

1950   The Inheritance of the Common Law by Richard
        O'Sullivan

1951   The Rational Strength of English Law by Professor
        F. H. Lawson

1952   English Law and the Moral Law by Professor A. L.
        Goodhart

1953   The Queen's Peace by Sir Carleton Kemp Allen

1954   Executive Discretion and Judicial Control by
        Professor C. J. Hamson

1955   The Proof of Guilt by Professor Glanville
        Williams

1956   Trial by Jury by the Rt Hon. Lord Devlin

1957   Protection from Power under English Law by the
        Rt Hon. Lord MacDermott

1958   The Sanctity of Contracts in English Law by
        Professor Sir David Hughes Parry

1959   Judge and Jurist in the Reign of Victoria by C. H.
        S. Fifoot

1960   The Common Law in India by M. C. Setalvad

1961   British Justice: The Scottish Contribution by
        Professor Sir Thomas Smith

1962   Lawyer and Litigant in England by the Rt Hon.
        Sir Robert Megarry

1963   Crime and the Criminal Law by the Baroness
        Wootton of Abinger

1964   Law and Lawyers in the United States by Dean Erwin N. Griswold

1965   New Law for a New World? by the Rt Hon. Lord Tangley

1966   Other People's Law by the Rt Hon. Lord Kilbrandon

1967   The Contribution of English Law to South African Law: and the Rule of Law in South Africa by the Hon. O. D. Schreiner

1968   Justice in the Welfare State by Professor H. Street

1969   The British Tradition in Canadian Law by the Hon. Bora Laskin

1970   The English Judge by Henry Cecil

1971   Punishment, Prison and the Public by Professor Sir Rupert Cross

1972   Labour and the Law by Professor Sir Otto Kahn-Freund

1973   Maladministration and its Remedies by Sir Kenneth Wheare

1974   English Law – the New Dimension by the Rt Hon. Lord Scarman

1975   The Land and the Development, or, The Turmoil and the Torment by Sir Desmond Heap

1976   The National Insurance Commissioners by Sir Robert Micklethwait

1977   The European Communities and the Rule of Law by Lord Mackenzie Stuart

1978   Liberty, Law and Justice by Professor Sir Norman Anderson

1979   Social History and Law Reform by Professor Lord McGregor of Durris

1980   Constitutional Fundamentals by Professor Sir William Wade

1981   Intolerable Inquisition? Reflections on the Law of
        Tax by Hubert Monroe

1982   The Quest for Security: Employees, Tenants, Wives
        by Professor Tony Honoré

1983   Hamlyn Revisited: The British Legal System Today
        by Lord Hailsham of St Marylebone

1984   The Development of Consumer Law and Policy –
        Bold Spirits and Timorous Souls by Sir Gordon
        Borrie

1985   Law and Order by Professor Ralf Dahrendorf

1986   The Fabric of English Civil Justice by Sir Jack
        Jacob

1987   Pragmatism and Theory in English Law by
        Professor P. S. Atiyah

1988   Justification and Excuse in the Criminal Law by
        Professor J. C. Smith

1989   Protection of the Public – A New Challenge by the
        Rt Hon. Lord Justice Woolf

1990   The United Kingdom and Human Rights by
        Dr Claire Palley

1991   Introducing a European Legal Order by Gordon
        Slynn

1992   Speech and Respect by Professor Richard Abel

1993   The Administration of Justice by Lord Mackay of
        Clashfern

1994   Blackstone's Tower: The English Law School by
        Professor William Twining

1995   From the Test Tube to the Coffin: Choice and
        Regulation in Private Life by the Hon. Mrs Justice
        Hale

1996   Turning Points of the Common law by the Rt Hon.
        the Lord Cooke of Thorndon

1997   Commercial Law in the Next Millennium by
        Professor Roy Goode

1998   Freedom, Law and Justice by the Rt Hon. Lord
        Justice Sedley

1999   The State of Justice by Professor Michael Zander
        QC

2000   Does the United Kingdom still have a Constitution?
        by Professor Anthony King

2001   Human Rights, Serious Crime and Criminal
        Procedure by Professor Andrew Ashworth QC

2002   Legal Conundrums in our Brave New World by
        Baroness Kennedy of the Shaws

2003   Judicial Activism by the Hon. Justice Michael Kirby
        AC, CMG

2004   Rights at Work: Global, European and British
        Perspectives by Sir Bob Hepple QC, FBA

2005   Can Human Rights Survive? by Professor Conor
        Gearty

2006   The Sovereignty of Law: The European Way by
        Sir Francis Jacobs KCMG, QC

2007   The Prisoners' Dilemma by Professor Nicola Lacey

2008   Judging Civil Justice by Dame Hazel Genn

2009   Widening Horizons: The Influence of Comparative
        Law and International Law on Domestic Law by
        Lord Bingham

2010   Lawyers and the Public Good: Democracy in
        Action? by Alan Paterson

2011   The Rule of Law and the Measure of Property by
        Jeremy Waldron

From Lord Denning, who gave the first of this series of lectures in 1949, to Jeremy Waldron in 2011, those who had previously been asked to deliver these three annual lectures have without exception been lawyers distinguished by their practice, their academic study or both.

For the 2012 series, the Trustees asked me. I started life as a lawyer, but I earned my living at the Bar for just two years before I was diverted into the preoccupation of the rest of my adult life, politics.

Whilst some, maybe many, political careers lightly brush our legal system if there is any contact with it at all, mine has followed a different course. I've been fascinated by the interaction of the work of our courts with the processes of government and the body politic. Over a significant part of my ministerial career I was responsible for an extensive legislative programme, including the Human Rights Act 1998, which has become a new foundation of what passes as the constitution of the United Kingdom.

The final ministerial post I held, from 2007 to 2010, was as Lord Chancellor – the first in modern times to sit in the House of Commons. No longer is the Lord Chancellor head of the judiciary – that role properly falls to the Lord Chief Justice. But the Lord Chancellor is responsible (indeed he or she has a statutory duty in this regard) for upholding the independence of the judiciary. The job gave me an interesting insight at the intersection of the three branches of modern democratic government – executive, judicial and legislative.

In alighting on subjects for my three lectures, I tried to identify subject areas where I could draw on my experiences over many years, and hopefully better illuminate aspects of our system.

Thus, the first lecture was on 'The future of the criminal courts'; the second on 'the Human Rights Act and Europe' and the third on 'Judicial appointments'.

I hope you enjoy them. I am very grateful to the Trustees for the honour they paid me in asking me to undertake this series.

JACK STRAW

1

The future of the criminal courts

It seems like the twinkling of an eye since I attended my initial
lectures as a first-year law student at the University of Leeds.
That was forty-eight years ago, in October 1964. Life was a
little different from today. Leeds United were then in the old
First Division – and in fact only just failed to top the table,
beaten by Manchester United on goal difference. The deci-
malisation of our currency was seven years away. A bus fare
into town cost one old penny. The environment was terrible.
My digs on the Burley Road were opposite a vinegar works
and a tannery. With back-to-back housing, the only place to
hang washing was across the street. The linen went grey in
the course of the day, a result of the smog which hung across
the Aire valley.

I came to the university on a full grant – £300 for the
whole year – and managed frugally, with just enough for
those priorities when you're eighteen: liquor, and the occa-
sional trip to Elland Road. But I was lucky. Just one in twelve
young people went to university, only a tiny handful from
backgrounds like mine. On our street on an Essex council
estate, my family was the only one whose children went onto
higher education. The university seemed very big. It had
6,000 students. It's five times that size today.

The Second World War, and its aftermath, touched
everything, defined everything. The Cold War, that existen-
tial struggle between the two superpowers, the United States

and the Soviet Union, was at its height. Nikita Khrushchev, the Soviet leader, was ousted in mid-October 1964, on the same night that Harold Wilson narrowly won a general election to return Labour to power after thirteen years in opposition.

The criminal justice system was different, too, and operated in a quite different social and political context. The three tiers of the criminal courts – magistrates, quarter sessions and assizes – would have been easily recognised by citizens from centuries before. There were six categories of offence.[1] The rigid division between solicitor and barrister was in place, the latter having a monopoly of advocacy in the higher courts. The number of lawyers in practice (in any area of law) was low compared with today: 2,500 practising barristers, and 32,000 practising solicitors in England and Wales, a quarter of the number in practice today.[2]

There were just 75,000 police officers in England and Wales – compared with 134,000 today – operating in 158 police forces, some with fewer than one hundred officers.[3] Leeds City had its own force, fiercely independent of the West Riding force lapping at its boundaries. These city (and borough) forces were run by the city council, with the chief

---

[1] Indictable only, summary only, indictable triable summarily with the defendant's consent, hybrid cases with and without a right to elect for trial by jury, summary cases in certain circumstances triable on indictment: see the 1975 James Committee report.

[2] Figures are from the early 1970s. There were 122,000 solicitors in practice in 2011 and 15,000 barristers in 2010.

[3] Royal Commission Report 1962 and Home Office Statistical Bulletin 09/12.

constable answerable to the chairman of the Watch Committee, one of the most powerful of municipal positions.

Crime was an issue, of course. It always has been, since it represents one extreme of human behaviour. The popular newspapers were filled then, as now, with lurid details of particularly horrible crimes. There were then, as now, periodic moral panics about the behaviour of the young. In the 1950s it had been over 'Teddy Boys' armed with flick-knives, a phenomenon which led to the first of a series of 'knife-crime' initiatives by ministers – this in the 1953 Prevention of Crime Act.[4] In the early 1960s the moral panic became intense, as 'Mods' on scooters and 'Rockers' on motorbikes wrecked seaside towns and battled with police officers for whom the only special riot equipment issued was dustbin lids.

Many similarities, but three significant differences about crime, between then and now.

First, there appeared simply to be less of it. In 1961 the crime figures recorded 107,000 larcenies, 36,000 offences of breaking and entering, 6,000 sex offences (which still included consensual gay sex), and 11,500 offences of violence against the person. The figures then and now are not strictly comparable, because of changes in definitions and reporting and recording practices. But the equivalent figures today show

- 477,200 robberies and motor thefts – up by a factor of 4;
- 489,100 burglaries – up by a factor of 13;

---

[4] The 1953 Prevention of Crime Act: an Act to prohibit the carrying of offensive weapons in public places without lawful authority or reasonable excuse.

3

- 52,200 sexual offences – up by a factor of 9; and
- 747,500 violence against the person offences – up by a stunning factor of 65.[5]

Employment levels, especially for that key group from which most offenders are drawn – unskilled young men – were relatively high. In July 1963, for example, total unemployment was 436,000, just under a sixth of the level today.[6] In the four years that I was a student at Leeds University, I never felt unsafe on the streets at night; security of student dwellings was light; and there were hard and soft drugs around, but their use was very much a minority activity. Their abuse was not the pervasive feature of so much crime, as it is today.

One indicator that there was 'less crime' was the prison population – 30,000 in England and Wales in 1962, compared with 85,000 and rising in 2012.[7]

I said that there 'appeared' to be less crime. Overall, there almost certainly was. But many crimes went unreported, or, if reported, unrecorded, and never investigated. The participants in pub fights, the men who routinely assaulted their wives, those who caused mayhem to their neighbours, abused vulnerable young women (and men) – all were generally ignored by the police and the system. Calling the police could be difficult enough. On my estate there was one telephone for

---

[5] Recorded crime figures for year to June 2012.
[6] 2.53 million: Office for National Statistics, Labour Market Statistics, October 2012.
[7] Ministry of Justice, monthly prison population statistics July, August, September 2012.

about a thousand people – in a box, typically with a queue outside. There were no offences relating to racism or homophobia, but gay sex, between consenting adults, remained a criminal offence.

The police and the courts were regarded, in general, as tough, not soft. There were no CCTV cameras, no iPhones with cameras and voice recorders. It was unwise to get involved in an altercation with the police. If you did, you could easily end up down a back alley, where you'd be 'taught a lesson', or charged; and when you got to court the magistrates would likely believe the officers, and not you, and add to your punishment for arguing with them, and the court.

The consequence of these two factors, of less crime, and greater public confidence in the system, was the third difference: that crime was nothing like the political hot potato it has become over the last twenty-five years. Yes, the manifestos did talk about the 'crime wave' – to quote from the Conservatives' 1966 manifesto, but 'law and order' was not the high-profile issue it was to become.

However, behind what now appears to have been a tranquil and ordered period, all was far from well. The police had done brilliantly to convey the impression, through the new media of television with series like *Dixon of Dock Green*, of a service replete with intelligence, sensitivity and high ethical standards. The propaganda masked a much uglier reality, of a police service which, especially in London and the other big cities, was endemically corrupt, and in which inducements and violence towards suspects were a substitute for proper forensic skills.

When I became Home Secretary in 1997, a very senior police officer sought to justify these practices of the past by claiming that it was 'noble cause corruption' – which led to effective law enforcement and relative peace on the streets. But even that was untrue. This 'noble cause corruption' meant that some gangs, of whom the Richardsons and Krays were only the most notorious, had some immunity from the police to operate as they wished; while those out of favour with the police or, to be more precise, not providing the police with favours, were dealt with harshly, or on occasions convicted of crimes which they had not committed. ('Fitted up' was the term.)

There was in those days no separate system for investigating complaints against the police. Occasionally, the Home Office and the Inspectorate felt compelled to move against some more egregious cases of abuse. But the leadership of the police was in general of a low quality, something compounded by an inability to recruit and retain bright people. When I became Home Secretary, the Chief Inspector of Constabulary told me that, in the two decades between 1945 and 1965, there had been fewer graduates recruited to the police than there had been years.

As Shadow Home Secretary in the mid 1990s, I toured Britain's police stations to gain a feel for the issues which were likely to land on my desk if I was lucky enough to take on the real job. At one police station in the East Midlands the Chief Superintendent told me how much he lamented that the 'Ways and Means Act' had been repealed. Bemused, I replied that I'd never ever come across this Act when I was studying law in the 1960s, or in practice at the Bar in the early 1970s.

What was the Act's date, what were its provisions, I asked? I was greeted with a condescending grin – and then an explanation that this was an Act that appeared in no law books – it was 'simply what we used to do'.

This senior police officer was not exaggerating. It is extraordinary to remind ourselves that until the passage of the Police and Criminal Evidence Act 1984,[8] there was – apart from habeas corpus – no statutory code to regulate the most fundamental of police powers, the arrest and detention of suspects. The only guidance was the non-statutory Judges' Rules. They were not the only powers of the state that were beyond the law. The tapping of telephones and other methods of intrusive surveillance, and the operation, indeed the very existence, of our intelligence and security agencies were outwith any statute.

Behind all this lay a comfortable, not to say a complacent, assumption that we were the nation that had so cherished and nurtured individual liberties – what we now call 'human rights' – that while we could codify and impose these on other nations, there was no need to do so for ourselves. Our natural decency, combined with a high-quality judiciary, skilled advocates and the democracy of the jury, would suffice. Thus it was British jurists who had largely drafted the European Convention on Human Rights, but the British political establishment (Labour included) resisted any idea that these rights needed to be incorporated into British law.

---

[8] First introduced in November 1982. Received Royal Assent 31 October 1984. For the most part came into force 1 January 1986.

Some change to our criminal justice system began in the late 1960s and 1970s. This included the introduction of majority verdicts (10–2) in jury trials, the reorganisation of the courts into two – magistrates' courts and Crown courts – in 1971, and the creation of the current classification of offences – indictable only, summary only, and 'either way' – under the 1977 Criminal Law Act.

But it took the emergence of a series of major scandals about the operation of the system in the early and mid 1970s, including the notorious Maxwell Confait case,[9] for the Prime Minister of the day, James Callaghan, to establish in 1978 a major Royal Commission on Criminal Procedure.[10] That reported in 1981 and led in turn to two major pieces of legislation, still on the statute book (though amended since): the Police and Criminal Evidence Act 1984 (PACE) and the Prosecution of Offenders Act 1985, which established the Crown Prosecution Service.

Curiously, PACE was the subject of intense party political controversy when the Bill was first introduced, with Labour eccentrically pledging that it would 'repeal [this] Bill [sic] because it infringes the rights and freedoms of the

---

[9] In 1972 Maxwell Confait, a male prostitute, was found dead following a fire. Three boys with learning difficulties were convicted variously of murder, manslaughter and arson. All three convictions were eventually quashed by the Court of Appeal. The case gave rise to serious questions about police procedures and how suspects were treated, especially children and those with learning difficulties.

[10] The Royal Commission on Criminal Procedure was established in February 1978 under the chairmanship of Professor Sir Cyril Philips. It issued its report in January 1981.

individuals'.[11] The fact that we did oppose the Bill (which had fallen with the 1983 general election, and had to be reintroduced after the election) reflects an almost eternal verity about reform of the criminal law and its procedure – that whenever even modest proposals are made, they meet very powerful resistance from those claiming that rights are being eroded, and (almost) that the end of civilisation may be nigh. Labour's problem in opposition, which continued until Tony Blair became our leader in 1994, was that it was too ready to act as the mouthpiece for pressure groups, rather than making its own decisions about what was in the public's interests.

The sound and fury notwithstanding, in most cases once the legislation has been passed the public has been able to see the reforms for what they are – sensible and measured – and the very same pressure groups who have been making their extravagant predictions abandon their campaign and move on to the next thing. Thus it was with majority verdicts, with the modification to the right of silence and other rules of evidence, with changes to the double-jeopardy rules, with judge-only trials where there has been jury nobbling, and much else. Sometimes, however, the opposition, especially in the House of Lords, is such as to kill a measure altogether.

That happened, as I discuss below, with the Mode of Trial Bill for which I was responsible as Home Secretary, and with provisions for judge-only trials in serious fraud cases.

I noted three differences in crime between the Britain of my law student days and the Britain of today. There are, in

---

[11] 1983 Labour Party manifesto.

9

addition, two major sets of changes which have fundamentally affected the environment in which the criminal justice system works.

The first is the effect of the technological revolution on the prevention and investigation of crime. The development of more and more sophisticated forensic techniques for matching DNA is the obvious example. It was this which led to the conviction in January 2012 of two of the suspects in the Stephen Lawrence case, although that could not have happened but for the modification of the once-hallowed rule of *ne bis in idem* – no one should be tried twice for the same offence. Call data – information about the origin and destination of voice and data traffic – is another example. CCTV is a third. It has had obvious utility in criminal trials but has impacted on the accountability of the police, too. Its fitting in custody suites, and police vans, has made these safer places for all concerned.

One of my jobs as Home Secretary was to act as the final appeal body for serious police discipline cases (not a role I thought was appropriate for a minister – I introduced legislation to change it). An early case that landed on my desk concerned a police inspector who had been accused of acting improperly in handling a female prisoner. The CCTV images confirmed this, graphically. The inspector had evidently always acted in this way – it was only when CCTV had been installed (of which he appeared unaware) that incontrovertible evidence against him became available.

The second important change has been the Human Rights Act 1998 (HRA). Its prospect led directly to the major reform and upgrading of investigatory powers by the state, contained in the Regulation of Investigatory Powers Act 2000 (RIPA). The fact that the sponsoring minister of any bill has to sign a 'section 19' certificate saying that the proposed legislation is, or is not, compliant with the European Convention on Human Rights has influenced the drafting of all bills.

The Act has not remotely been a 'villain's charter' as alleged by some sections of the popular press. Indeed, as Keir Starmer pointed out in an important lecture in 2009, its provisions have, rather, benefited victims, and made the whole of the system much more alert to their needs.[12] It appears to have directly affected the criminal trial process much less than has sometimes been suggested, not least because our system is so obviously compliant with the obligations under Article 6 of the Convention in any event.

That said, a dozen years after the Act came into force, we can see that it led to that 'culture of human rights' that was one of the key objectives for those of us who backed the incorporation of Convention rights into UK law.

We do not have a written constitution which provides protections for the individual against the overweening power of the state, and by which a Supreme Court can declare primary legislation to be unconstitutional, and therefore inoperative. But part of the success – and it has been a success – of the Human Rights Act has been the way in which it works with the grain of our constitutional arrangements, at the heart of which is parliamentary sovereignty. Thus the higher courts can declare primary legislation to be 'incompatible' with Convention articles, but by the same Act those provisions

---

[12] Public Prosecution Service Annual Lecture, 2009.

stay in force unless and until Parliament decides to amend or repeal them. In practice, successive governments, and parliaments, have sought very rapidly to bring legislation into compatibility with the Convention decisions of our courts. A positive respect for human rights is now embedded in the collective consciousness of the nation, as well as in the law.

I want at this stage to consider some changes in the use of juries in our criminal courts.

The jury is a fundamental part not just of our criminal justice system, but of the rule of law, and of our democracy.

The fact that decisions in all serious criminal cases are made by twelve citizens, chosen by ballot, gives huge strength to the whole of our system of law. There is the widest possible consent to the verdicts that juries hand down; an acceptance that if a jury determines that someone is guilty, they are. And there has been a good deal in the argument that juries were the last line of defence against arbitrary government, or the abuse of power.

Baroness Helena Kennedy, herself a leading silk, put the case for juries in these terms:

> Juries keep the law honest and comprehensible because working with juries – as those of us who work with juries know – puts an obligation on all of us to explain the law and the rules and to apply the standards of the public to what is right and wrong. The jury stops the law becoming opaque. It stops the law becoming closed and sometimes even dishonest ... The jury, in fact, protects the judiciary. It is what maintains the esteem of the British judiciary.[13]

[13] HL Debates, 15 July 2003, cols. 779–80.

But the centrality of juries in our system cannot mean that the exact boundary between those matters that should go for jury trial, and those that could and should better be dealt with by judges or magistrates alone, should be set in concrete for all time. It has never been. And the fact that, under the Human Rights Act, our courts are even more attentive to the individual's rights, and to preventing abuse of those rights by the state, should, I hope, provide for a calmer atmosphere when considering changes to the trial system. If juries were once the last line of defence against arbitrary government, I suggest that line is now held by the Human Rights Act.

In recent years there have been three sets of proposals to shift the boundary – in respect of jury nobbling, either-way cases and fraud trials.

The first of these has been brought into force. To date there has been only one judge-only trial – in the case of *R* v. *Twomey and others* in 2010. Three previous trials of the same defendants had collapsed, because of evidence, which the Court of Appeal accepted, that in the earlier trials the juries had been nobbled. At the judge-only trial there were predictable protests outside the court by friends of the defendants that 'No Jury = No Justice', to quote from the placards, but I have heard no one, once the dust had settled on their conviction and sentence, suggest that justice had not been done. The injustice arose from the actions of the criminals concerned to interfere with the integrity of the juries – actions which would have been successful but for this provision.

The second and third proposals were both passed in the House of Commons, but thwarted in the House of Lords. Both in my view continue to have merit, and need to be revived.

The jurisdiction of England and Wales is unusual among common law jurisdictions in giving defendants a choice of court where they have been charged with middling offences, such as theft or actual bodily harm.

A decade after the Philips Royal Commission reported in 1981, another Royal Commission was established, this one in the wake of some serious miscarriages of justice, including the Birmingham Six. Chaired by Viscount Runciman, the members of the Royal Commission on Criminal Justice included the distinguished human rights lawyer, Michael Zander. They concluded, unanimously, as follows:

> We do not think that defendants should be able to choose their court of trial solely on the basis that they think that they will get a fairer hearing at one level than the other ... Nor in our view should defendants be entitled to choose the mode of trial which they think will offer them a better chance of acquittal any more than they should be able to choose the judge who they think will give them the most lenient sentence. Loss of reputation is a different matter, since jury trial has long been regarded as appropriate for cases involving that issue. But it should only be one of the factors to be taken into account and will often be relevant only to first offenders ... Under our proposed scheme ... it would be for the bench to weigh up all the factors and determine the mode of trial. We see merit in the legislation specifically referring to the various matters (including potential loss of reputation) which the bench should take into account.[14]

[14] Royal Commission on Criminal Justice 1993, Cm 2263, p. 88.

The case they made seemed to me to be overwhelming – unless, that is, the opponents of any change were arguing that the quality of justice meted out by the magistrates' courts was fundamentally defective. If they were, those opponents should have come forward with proposals for root and branch reform of the magistrates' courts, for, after all, some of the summary-only offences they deal with – such as drink driving, or assault on a police officer – can be just as reputationally disastrous as some either-way offences. But the opponents never had the gall, and still less the evidence, to argue this. As Runciman pointed out, defendants who feel they have been wrongly convicted in the magistrates' court have an absolute right of a retrial (before a judge and two magistrates), a facility not available after a conviction by a jury.

I sought to implement this proposal of Runciman in my Mode of Trial Bill 1999. In a momentary loss of attention, I made a fatal mistake over its parliamentary handling. I agreed that it should start in the Lords. Normally this doesn't matter. But the Parliament Acts, which give the Commons the power to override a Lords' veto of a bill, only operate in respect of bills which start in the Commons. The bill was scuppered in the Lords, with the legal profession – over-represented in the Lords, and ready to serve its own interests in a way that would make the same people howl if any other group were doing this (bankers, say) – whipping itself into a frenzy. Catherine Bennett, a columnist for the *Guardian*, acidly observed at the time: 'Asking barristers to comment on trial by jury is like asking pigs what they think about troughs'.[15] A No. 2 Bill,

[15] *Guardian*, 1 August 1998.

which started in the Commons, was passed by a large majority there, but failed again in the Lords, and the whole project hit the buffers with the 2001 general election.

Meanwhile, the Court of Appeal judge Sir Robin Auld had been asked in late 1999 by the Lord Chancellor, the Attorney General and me to look at the efficiency and effectiveness of the court system. His report, the Auld Review,[16] was published in October 2001. He proposed a unified criminal court system, with three tiers – magistrates, district and crown. Like Runciman, he proposed that the defendant should no longer have a right to choose the court to try him or her; instead, that should be a matter for a district judge. Anxious because of my experiences, my successors in the Home Office decided not to pursue this. The then opposition parties, determined to develop a narrative that we were undermining hallowed British freedoms, then committed themselves to no change to access to jury trial.

Except, except. What the current administration has done (to echo a phrase of von Clausewitz) is to implement Runciman and Auld by 'other means'. A little-noticed change in the legal aid rules was brought in late in 2011, that where magistrates have determined that they should hear an either-way case, but the defendant nonetheless elects for jury trial at Crown court, and later pleads guilty, then legal aid is paid only at the lower, magistrates' court rates. What is fascinating is that those who brought in this change used arguments

---

[16] Rt Hon. Lord Justice Auld, *Review of the Criminal Courts of England and Wales* (London: Stationary Office, October 2001).

identical to those which Runciman used, and which I used for my Mode of Trial Bill, which they opposed.[17]

I supported this change in the legal aid rules. But it's second best. On any analysis, it is far less acceptable than giving the court the right to decide venue. What this rule change means is that the supposed 'higher quality' of the Crown court continues to be available for those with a deep pocket, for the well-off, but not for the vast majority of defendants. Is that just?

The other proposal for non-jury trials which hit the buffers was in respect of serious fraud. Lord Roskill's Fraud Trials Committee recommended in 1986 that serious and complex fraud cases should be heard by a special tribunal comprising a judge and specially qualified lay members. Lord Justice Auld's 2001 Report said that the arguments in favour of replacing trial by judge and jury with some other form of tribunal in these cases had become more pressing since the Roskill Committee, 'given the ever-lengthening and complexity of fraud trials and their increasingly specialised nature and international ramifications'.[18] The government's response was to try to provide, in the 2003 Criminal Justice Act, for serious and complex fraud cases to be heard by a judge only.

---

[17] For example, 'The Government's view [is] that it is inappropriate in this narrow group of cases (which the magistrates' court has determined to be of a level of seriousness and complexity suitable for them to be dealt with summarily) for the taxpayer to continue to pay significantly more for a guilty plea by reason of the venue in which the plea takes place.' Ministry of Justice, Reform of Legal Aid in England and Wales: the Government Response, Cm 8072, June 2011, pp. 50–2.

[18] Auld, *Review of the Criminal Courts of England and Wales*, para. 182.

Defeated – again – in the Lords, David Blunkett saved the measure by promising that it would only be commenced by affirmative order of both houses. An attempt at such commencement, and a further attempt at primary legislation, were both blocked in the Lords. Section 43 of the Criminal Justice Act 2003 remained dormant on the statute books until it was repealed by the Protection of Freedoms Act 2012.

The arguments for judge-only trials in such cases seem to me to be pretty overwhelming. It is not about whether juries have the intelligence to try such cases. They do. It is whether it is reasonable to ask a cross-section of citizens to give up months of their personal and working lives for a single case. Can we hope that twelve people who can do so will form a representative cross-section of the community?

And we need to understand this. There is a rough correspondence between the number of burglaries, robberies and assaults, and the number of cases for those offences brought to trial. There is no such correspondence when it comes to fraud; rather, I perceive, an ever-widening gap between the incidence of the offence and its prosecution. This is a time of flagrant abuses within the financial sector, and when fraud is becoming the crime of choice in the organised criminal world. The relative paucity of fraud cases brought to a successful conclusion reflects instead the obvious problems of bringing these cases to trial within the existing system. The response of Parliament and government has, again, been to use 'other means' to deal with fraud and other financial irregularity. These other means are through astonishingly pervasive powers granted to the regulatory authorities to investigate, and to sanction wrongdoing by the imposition of fines on individuals and corporations, public censure and prohibitions on working within the financial sector. But these sanctions, though essential, are insufficient for dealing with fraud, where the criminal law should be used much more extensively. I should add that an associated area which the courts need better to address is how they handle applications under the Proceeds of Crime Act 2002.

I didn't spend my entire time as Home Secretary and then Lord Chancellor banging my head against the brick wall of Mode of Trial. I was much more successful in working with the judges to bring about changes in the area of sentencing.

That this was possible at all was in part a symptom of a wider change – in the relationship between the judiciary, Whitehall and Parliament in the running of the criminal courts. The judiciary is, rightly, jealous of its independence. I always sought to uphold that independence, no matter how irritating or inconvenient I found the judges or their judgments. But I didn't think – still don't – that ruled out the possibility of the judiciary, Parliament and the government working together to improve the system.

Until the 1990s the senior judiciary was very resistant to any kind of intervention by anybody outside the judiciary in the running of the courts. Their effectiveness, their efficiency, and their sentencing powers, were all matters for the judges and the judges alone. When I became Home Secretary in 1997 this had started to change, but my relationship with the then Lord Chief Justice Lord Bingham, while good by the standards of the time, was a formal and slightly stilted one.

Flash forwards fifteen years, and we now have a situation where the Lord Chief Justice appears before the Justice

Select Committee; the Board of HM Courts and Tribunal Service has a lay chair and is populated by a mixture of senior judges and senior Court Service executives; and there is a much greater readiness throughout the judiciary to accept that they are responsible for ensuring that time and money within the courts system are properly used.

On sentencing, the situation in 1997 when I became Home Secretary was that while the Court of Appeal had issued many guidelines over the decades, there was nonetheless too much variation between courts in the sentences they handed down for identical kinds of offending behaviour and offender. My aim was to inform the public, practitioners, victims and offenders alike about the sentences (including non-custodial ones) likely to be handed down for a specific range of offending behaviour. The Crime and Disorder Act dipped a tentative toe in the water, with the creation of a Sentencing Advisory Panel. It did good work. Six years later, in 2003, David Blunkett built on this with the establishment of the Sentencing Guidelines Council, placing a duty on the courts to take account of the detailed advice they would lay down. Back in charge of this area as Justice Secretary, I completed the work by merging the two bodies into a Sentencing Council with clearer, stronger powers, chaired by a senior judge, with distinguished members on it, and a formal role for Parliament, through the Justice Select Committee.[19] The system – which always had cross-party support – is now an established part of the criminal justice landscape.

[19] Coroners and Justice Act 2009.

These changes have led to greater predictability in sentencing, but there is a still a problem about 'judicial continuity' in the management of offenders. Although section 178 of the Criminal Justice Act 2003 gave magistrates' courts the power to bring back before them offenders sentenced to community orders, to review how well they were complying, the effectiveness of this approach relies on the offender being brought back before the same magistrate who handed down the original sentence. There is some good innovative work going on in this area, but it needs to be extended.[20] It will also be interesting to see what, if any, impact the 'payment by results' schemes for prisons (which I piloted and which the current government is extending) has on sentencing practice, including judicial continuity in the management of offenders.

The lecture on which this chapter is based was chaired in Leeds by Keir Starmer. Not least because of this great honour, I need to say something about the service over which Mr Starmer presides. I start by saying how brilliantly Mr Starmer has carried out his role running this high-profile service.

The Crown Prosecution Service (CPS) arose from that landmark 1981 Royal Commission on Criminal Procedure I discussed above. I have found it instructive, in preparing for this lecture, to look back at what the Commission said. It noted how ramshackle the existing prosecution arrangements were; that they varied from police force to police force. It noted that some police forces used private solicitors to

---

[20] See www.criminaljusticealliance.org/MAnationalenquiryNov11.pdf.

conduct their prosecutions (two of those forces were British Transport Police and Surrey Constabulary; the firm they used regularly instructed me). Clearly, change was needed. But what is really interesting, reading back thirty years on, is that the Philips Royal Commission said that the last thing the government should do was to establish a national service. 'Our conclusion is that ... a centrally directed national prosecution system for England and Wales is neither desirable nor necessary and we do not recommend its establishment.'[21]

This was, nonetheless, what the then government did. Chiefly, it was about ensuring ministerial accountability, a clear chain of command. And – although the Royal Commission's concerns about the bureaucracy and other problems inherent in a national system were prescient – there is no point in pulling the organisation up by its roots now.

But are there more incremental reforms that might be considered, I wonder, with a greater degree of regional autonomy? A sensible place to start might be Wales and perhaps one non-London English region. Wales is, and should remain, part of our single jurisdiction. But some parts of the courts system, such as the Children and Family Court Advisory and Support Service (Cafcass), already operate satisfactorily in the Principality with a high degree of regional autonomy, and there is no reason why we could not look at a similar arrangement for the prosecution service. A more autonomous Welsh CPS could meet the aspirations of the Welsh people for their

---

[21] Report of the Royal Commission on Criminal Procedure, 1981, Cmnd 8092, para. 7.24.

country and, importantly, provide some lessons about how this might work in other areas.

I also want to discuss the quality of advocacy. It is great that Mr Starmer has encouraged his prosecutors to take on a much more public role, and that he has continued to ensure that consideration of the victims of crime is deeply embedded in their culture. Both of these were notably absent from the prosecutorial culture thirty to forty years ago. But I was very struck, as I talked to leading defence lawyers in preparing this material, that when I asked them what single thing they would change to improve the operation of the courts – and this is successful defence lawyers we are talking about – they called for more resources for prosecutors.

Mr Starmer, I am sure, would say that he is managing on his money, because that is what a good public servant has to say. My view is that funding put into the CPS, to improve both the quality of its advocacy and the resources available to support its prosecutors, would pay for itself in reduced delays in court, and more early guilty pleas.

It's not only prosecutors – the variable quality of advocacy is a problem among defence lawyers as well, a problem that the Quality Assurance Scheme for Advocates, due to be in place in 2013, recognises, and which I hope meets the expectations riding on it. Behind the current anxieties about the variable quality of advocates is a much bigger issue – that, in my view, the system is producing too many lawyers who are chasing too few jobs, a situation which is bound to get worse, not better.

As I sought to spell out at the opening of this chapter, there never was a golden age for our criminal courts, nor

23

some mythical time when there was a bobby on the beat on every street corner ready to give young offenders a clip round the ear, and when older offenders 'came quietly' with the confession that it was 'a fair cop, guv'. In truth, our criminal justice system – from the police through to sentencers – is more effective, more professional, more replete with integrity, and more focused on the needs of victims than at any other point in my lifetime. But this has only happened by a programme of reform. As I have suggested here, that is a programme which is far from at an end.

2

The Human Rights Act and Europe

In this chapter I want to consider the relationship between the Human Rights Act, our courts and the British Parliament on the one hand, and the European Court of Human Rights in Strasbourg and the Council of Europe on the other. I will be arguing:

- That the Human Rights Act has been a resounding success. It is here to stay. It is not the problem, rather part of the solution to a fundamental impediment to the operation of democratic politics across Europe: namely, the ever-widening jurisdiction of the European Court in Strasbourg, for which there is neither authority in the treaties, nor popular consent.
- That our higher courts should have the confidence to come to their own interpretations of rights under the European Convention on Human Rights, without having automatically to follow Strasbourg's jurisprudence. Here I come down strongly on the side of those such as Lord Irvine of Lairg, former Lord Chancellor, and Baroness Hale, Justice of the UK Supreme Court, in their rejection of the 'mirror' principle set out in a series of leading cases, starting with *Alconbury*[1] and *Ullah*.[2]

---

[1] *R (on the application of Alconbury Developments Ltd) v. Secretary of State for the Environment, Transport and the Regions,* [2001] UKHL 23; [2003] 2 AC 295.

[2] *R (Ullah) v. Special Adjudicator,* [2004] UKHL 26; [2004] 2 AC 323.

- That encouraging our higher courts to come to their own, more independent, conclusions is not an invitation to them to stray into areas which should properly be resolved by political process, nor is there any evidence that they would do so.
- That the Strasbourg Court needs to rein in its scope so as to revert to its founding purpose: the protection of those basic human rights, the abuse of which during the Second World War was the reason for its establishment.
- That there is no democratic state in the world where decisions of that state's highest court cannot be modified, or abrogated, by a mechanism which ultimately reflects the will of the people – a 'democratic override'. In contrast, the Strasbourg Court is establishing itself as a Supreme Court for Europe without any democratic override whatsoever. The reason there is no such override is that the treaties never anticipated this vastly expanded role for the Court. The parliaments of European Union member states have explicitly signed up for the jurisdiction of the European Court of Justice (ECJ). No such explicit authority exists for Strasbourg. The failure of the Strasbourg Court to understand this is contrary, among much else, to the purposes of Article 3 of Protocol 1 of the Convention. This requires the member states 'to hold free elections at reasonable intervals by secret ballot, under conditions which will ensure the free expression of the opinion of the people in the choice of the legislature'. If those legislatures cannot then give expression to the will of the people because the Strasbourg Court says so, democracy itself is undermined.
- That this determination by Strasbourg gratuitously to expand its jurisdiction, and to fail to provide a very wide

'margin of appreciation', save over the protection of basic human rights, was bound at some stage to lead to conflict with the people's will in one or other member state. The fact that the current best example of this conflict is with the UK Parliament over prisoner voting rights is incidental. The prospect of conflict is now inherent within the approach of the Strasbourg Court.

- That the responsibility for this conflict lies with Strasbourg; so must its solution. The UK Parliament should not be persuaded to move away from the people's will by threats that 'there be dragons' unless the people concede to Strasbourg.
- Strasbourg will be the loser if it continues its present approach. Human rights in the United Kingdom will continue to be protected by the Human Rights Act, as interpreted by our courts.

Chapter 12 of my recently published memoirs, *Last Man Standing*, is entitled 'A Tale of Two Policies'. It compares the conception, birth and childhood of two landmark and parallel pieces of legislation passed in the first parliament of the 1997–2010 Labour administration – the Freedom of Information Act (FOIA), and the Human Rights Act (HRA).

For a variety of reasons, which I set out at length in that chapter, the preparation and implementation of the FOIA was not a happy experience; the consequences of these inadequacies show to this day.

The contrast with the HRA was and is stark. The three years of Tony Blair's service as Leader of the Opposition, from 1994 to 1997, were by far the most intellectually invigorating and rigorous the Labour Party has seen in the past five decades.[3] We really worked hard in the pre-1997 period, challenging and stress-testing bright ideas to ensure that the designs could be brought to fruition: that, as it were, the planes would fly, not nosedive into the sea. On no project that I was involved in was that more true than the Human Rights Act.

Scepticism about the idea of incorporation of the Convention into UK law had been endemic within the British political class – both sides – ever since the founding treaty had been drafted. An attempt by the Conservative MP and lawyer, Edward Gardner QC, in 1987, to bring in a bill of incorporation, was still-born, defeated by both front-benches. Aside from the argument that we did not need incorporation, the elephant in the room was parliamentary sovereignty. There was no appetite for giving our senior judges the power to declare primary law passed by Parliament unconstitutional and invalid, and, equally, no clear idea about how this impediment could be overcome.

Many were involved in identifying a solution, way beyond the party faithful. The structure of our bill was debated in a Liberal Democrat/Labour working party chaired by Robert Maclennan[4] and the late Robin Cook. Leading academics, including Professor Francesca Klug[5] and Robert

---

[3] The only comparable period was the planning for the post-war period which took place under the aegis of Churchill's coalition government while the bloody conflict was still raging, and which found its way into Labour's 1945 manifesto.

[4] Then MP for Caithness, Sutherland and Easter Ross, now Baron Maclennan of Rogart.

[5] Professor Francesca Klug OBE, now Professorial Research Fellow at the LSE and former independent academic advisor to the government.

Hazell,[6] were hugely helpful in the detailed consideration they gave to the squaring of various circles. Not least because of the work we had undertaken, and published, in opposition,[7] when we came into government we found that some of the brightest officials, government lawyers and parliamentary draftsmen in Whitehall had been applying their minds to the issue with great thoroughness and imagination for many months, and would continue to do so.

Happily, at its outset the bill was controversial – which meant that there was a proper engagement on its detail, rather than the mush which is the almost inevitable by-product of bills on which there is a prior consensus. Equally satisfactory, at the conclusion of all the debates, there was agreement on the bill, precisely because of the improvements that were made on it during its passage through both houses.

The result was an Act which was elegantly crafted, and which has met the test of time. The Act has been a success. Gradually, it has dawned on its erstwhile opponents that if there is a problem with the Convention it lies not in the British courts' approach to it, but in Strasbourg.

That is illustrated by thinking through the consequences of repealing the HRA while remaining within the Council of Europe and the Convention. Doing so would propel us back to the pre-HRA days, in which our judiciary and courts could have no input into the development of

---

[6] Professor of British Politics and Government and Director of the Constitution Unit, University College London.

[7] See, for example, Jack Straw MP and Paul Boateng MP, 'Bringing Rights Home', consultation paper, December 1996.

jurisprudence on the Convention because the Convention articles were not incorporated into British law, while we would still be subject to decisions of the Strasbourg Court – the worst of both worlds, not the best. As I often had to remind those who were sceptical about the HRA, some of the most controversial European Court of Human Rights decisions that have affected the United Kingdom were made before, not after, 2 October 2000, when the HRA came into force – decisions such as *Chahal* v. *UK*[8] and *McCann* v. *UK*.[9] In none of those cases could the Strasbourg Court have benefited from the opinions of our senior jurists, since the latter were denied that role.

Since the passage of the Act, it has not been judgments of the UK courts on Convention interpretations that have caused real difficulty (and not to say incomprehension), but those of Strasbourg. Of course there have been judgments of our senior courts here which have been inconvenient to the government of the day – including the government in which I served. In a society which prides itself on that separation of powers so crucial to the effectiveness of a democratic government, the courts would not, could not, be doing their job if their decisions were not sometimes inconvenient to the state. If the courts cannot speak truth to power, they are nothing. But we are blessed in this country with a judiciary of the highest quality; moreover, because it comes from us, our society, it is acutely sensitive to the cultural and political norms of our society. Since incorporation via the HRA, the

---

[8] *Chahal* v. *United Kingdom*, no. 70/1995/576/662, European Court of Human Rights, 15 November 1996.
[9] *McCann* v. *United Kingdom*, (1996) 21 EHRR 97.

judiciary's decisions on the Convention have, as one would expect, gone with the grain of those norms – as its judgments in *Marper*,[10] *Hirst*[11] and *Al-Khawaja*[12] well illustrate.

We knew what we were saying in the bill; meant what we said. By 'we' I mean not least Lord Irvine of Lairg, the Lord Chancellor at the time, and me – the twin 'midwives' of the bill, in the Lords and the Commons. There was nothing sloppy or accidental about its drafting.

Section 1 states quite simply that the 'Convention rights' – that is, the Articles set out in Schedule 1 – are 'to have effect for the purposes of this Act'.[13] This language, of incorporation of the key articles of the Convention, could not be clearer or less ambiguous. This section is, at it were, about the Holy Texts, the Ten Commandments, the Sermon on the Mount, the word of the Holy Prophet in the Koran.

But what, then, of the commentaries – the Torah, the writings of the saints, papal encyclicals, the Hadith – how were they to be treated?

Parliament gives its answer in section 2, and the language could not be more different from that of section 1. To the extent that ('so far as') a court or tribunal believes that it is relevant to the question before it, then it 'must take into account' four categories of texts. These four include not only

---

[10] *S. and Marper* v. *United Kingdom*, nos. 30562/04 and 30566/04, European Court of Human Rights, 4 December 2008.

[11] *Hirst* v. *United Kingdom (No. 2)*, (2004) 38 EHRR 40; no. 74025/01, GC, European Court of Human Rights, 6 October 2005.

[12] *Al-Khawaja and Tahery* v. *United Kingdom*, no. 26766/05, [2011] ECHR 2127 (15 December 2011).

[13] S. 1(2) HRA.

judgments of the Strasbourg Court, and advisory opinions, but opinions of the European Commission on Human Rights, and decisions by the Commission or the Council of Ministers.[14]

The fact that all four groups of text are treated in the same way in the same section is the first clue, if one were needed, that Parliament was not intending that any of these texts should be treated by the British courts as Holy Writ. The judgments of the Grand Chamber of the Court are, on the whole, carefully argued judicial documents; but opinions and decisions of the Commission are much more political in character, and those of the Council of Ministers wholly political.

The second clue, hardly a clue at all since it's there in black letters, comes from the key words of the section – 'must *take into account*'.[15] They were chosen with care.

Lord Irvine gave an important lecture on 'A British Interpretation of Convention Rights' late last year, whose content I entirely endorse.[16] In it, he said that these words of section 2 'can be paraphrased to "have regard to", "consider", "treat as relevant", "bear in mind"'.

We did not say 'must follow', not even with the qualification 'the clear and constant jurisprudence of the European Court';[17] still less did we say that the British courts must 'mirror' the terms of these decisions and other texts emanating from Strasbourg. While we most certainly anticipated

---

[14] S. 2(1)(a–d) HRA.   [15] Emphasis added.

[16] UCL Judicial Institute, 14 December 2011.

[17] *R (Alconbury)* v. *Secretary of State for Environment, Transport and the Regions*, [2003] 2 AC 295, at para. 26, *per* Lord Slynn.

that the British courts would wish to keep up to date with Strasbourg jurisprudence, we certainly did not say, nor did we ever intend, that their duty was to 'keep pace with [this] jurisprudence ... no more, but certainly no less' to quote Lord Bingham in *Ullah*,[18] nor, equally, 'no less, but certainly no more' to quote Lord Brown in *Al-Skeini*.[19]

Instead, as we spelt out in our White Paper, one argument in favour of incorporation was to enable British judges 'to make a distinctively British contribution to the development of the jurisprudence of human rights in Europe'.[20]

In some respects our senior judiciary have indeed met this expectation. But they have been unnecessarily constrained from properly fulfilling this task by a series of decisions by the law lords and now the UK Supreme Court, which have, frankly, changed the meaning of section 2 from 'take account of' to 'follow'.

This series starts with *Alconbury* and runs through *Ullah*, *Al-Skeini* and *AF (No. 3)*[21] to the unanimous Supreme Court judgment in *Pinnock*.[22] The summation of this approach is called by its advocates the 'mirror principle' – that our courts should, wherever they can, mirror the decisions of Strasbourg.

Some of the finest judicial minds in the country have come down in favour of this approach, as Sir Philip Sales

[18] *R (Ullah)* v. *Special Adjudicator*, [2004] UKHL 26.
[19] *R (on application of Al-Skeini)* v. *Ministry of Defence*, [2007] UKHL 26.
[20] White Paper, 'Rights Brought Home: The Human Rights Bill', 1997, Cm 3782, para. 1.14.
[21] *Secretary of State for the Home Department* v. *F*, [2009] UKHL 28.
[22] *Pinnock* v. *Manchester City Council*, [2011] UKSC 6.

recites in his spirited response to Lord Irvine's views.[23] Challenging this approach may be deemed as well above the pay grade of someone like me, who is no jurist. But challenge it I do, as one of the two senior ministers responsible for the Act and as someone who has taken the closest possible interest in its working since then.

In making that challenge I am comforted to know that on the same side are many fine judicial minds. Lord Judge, our Lord Chief Justice, is one;[24] Baroness Hale, a justice of the Supreme Court, is another.[25]

In her lecture, 'Is the Supreme Court Supreme?', given in December 2011, Lady Hale took the mirror principle apart. She explained that the HRA 'does not require us to follow the Strasbourg jurisdiction', that there is 'nothing in the Act, or in its purposes, to say that we should deliberately go no further than Strasbourg has gone, or that we should refrain from devising what we think is the right result in a case where Strasbourg has not yet spoken'. She repeats with approval what I said in the Commons, expanding on the section of the White Paper I quoted earlier, saying that,

[23] Philip Sales, 'Strasbourg Jurisprudence and the Human Rights Act: A Response to Lord Irvine', [2012] *Public Law* 253.

[24] 'There has been a tendency to follow much more closely than I think we should ... I think there is a realisation of that and I think judges generally are aware of this and are examining decisions of the European court that much more closely to see whether what you can spell out of it is a principle or just a facts-specific decision.' Lord Judge, giving evidence to the Joint Parliamentary Committee on Human Rights, 15 November 2011.

[25] 'Argentoratum Locutum: Is the Supreme Court Supreme?', Nottingham Human Rights Lecture 2011, 1 December 2011.

'through incorporation we are giving a profound margin of appreciation to British courts to interpret the Convention in accordance with British jurisprudence as well as European jurisprudence'.[26] She criticises the 'amount of time [which] counsel spend [before the UK Supreme Court] ... discussing the Strasbourg case law' – a problem, I might add, which arises directly from the errors of *Ullah* and *Alconbury*. These counsel, says Baroness Hale, treat Strasbourg case law 'as if it were the case law of our domestic courts'. 'This is odd,' she continues, '... because Strasbourg case law is not like ours. It is not binding upon anyone, even upon them. They have no concepts of *ratio decidendi* and *stare decisis*. Their decisions are at best an indication of the broad approach which Strasbourg will take to a particular problem.'[27]

Then Baroness Hale delivers her *coup de grâce*: 'A fourth reason to doubt the mirror principle is that the reason given for it, in *Ullah* and elsewhere, does not make much sense.'

Part of the convoluted argument that the Baroness so correctly derides is that 'there is a risk' that the contracting parties may 'by judicial interpretation become bound by obligations which they did not expressly accept and might not have been willing to accept'.[28]

The late Lord Bingham, who made this observation, was right to worry about the ever-expanding remit of the Strasbourg Court for which it has no mandate. It's a concern

---

[26] HC Deb., Vol. 313, col. 424 (3 June 1998).
[27] 'Argentoratum Locutum', 4.
[28] *Brown* v. *Stott*, [2003] 1 AC 681, *per* Lord Bingham.

I share; it forms a central part of my criticism of that court, with which I deal later in this lecture. But that consideration is irrelevant to the question as to whether our courts should free themselves from their self-imposed shackles by a rewriting of section 2, and interpret the Convention articles in the way they judge best. In fact, it's odd that it is Lord Bingham's approach, not its reverse, which is most likely to achieve what he said he feared.

The arguments against giving our courts the freedom of interpretation intended by section 2 include these two:

First, that to do so would be to create greater uncertainty about the law. 'The HRA is not intended to allow for or to produce random and arbitrary differences between courts and tribunals in their interpretation of Convention rights', to quote Sir Philip Sales again.[29] We do not, however, need the mirror principle to protect us from this mischief. Precisely because of those twin pillars of our common law jurisdiction, *stare decisis* and *ratio decidendi*, our courts and tribunals are models of consistency and predictability, whether in areas covered by the Convention or those quite outwith its scope. (These twin pillars are among the many reasons, by the way, that so many international companies with no ethnic or territorial connection with the United Kingdom choose to have their contracts subject to arbitration under English law.)

The second is that if the British courts allowed themselves freer rein over the interpretation of Convention rights, they might usurp Parliament's rights to make and to change the law.

---

[29] Sales, 'Strasbourg Jurisprudence', 258.

Let me take on here a charge that I am at best being paradoxical, but, more likely, contrary, in arguing for greater freedom for the British courts, while saying (as I do) that the Strasbourg Court has significantly to pull back from the jurisdictional expansion it has made in recent decades.

There is nothing contradictory in my approach. Regardless of how they interpret Convention rights, our British courts cannot and do not challenge the most fundamental foundation of our system of democracy, that of parliamentary sovereignty. Parliament is supreme.

One of the many virtues of our courts, going back centuries before the HRA, is that they have sought to defend the individual against the arbitrary or oppressive power of the state. To do so they have, among other things, exploited any ambiguity of language in statutes to ensure, for example, that individuals, however 'undeserving' they may be, are not left completely destitute. They did so in the mid 1990s[30] – way before the HRA was even a gleam in the eye – and much more recently in the 2005 decision of the law lords in *Limbuela*.[31] In that case the court held that it was inhuman and degrading treatment to deny some categories of asylum seeker both the right to earn a living and the right to any assistance from the state, and so to reduce them to utter destitution.

This was one of those decisions of our courts which could be classed as inconvenient to the executive. I recall that it

[30] In 1997, in *R* v. *Westminster City Council and others, ex p. M., P., A. and X,* [1997] 1 CCLR 85. §.

[31] *R (Limbuela)* v. *Secretary of State for the Home Department,* [2005] UKHL 66.

caused quite a stir at the time. But if we – the executive – had decided to ask Parliament to pass primary legislation which said in plain, unambiguous terms that certain categories of asylum seeker were indeed to be rendered destitute, and Parliament had agreed, that would have been that so far as the British courts were concerned. The section 19 certificate might well have had to say that in the sponsoring minister's opinion he was 'unable to make a statement of compatibility' regarding the proposed legislation, but that is a situation anticipated by the Act;[32] and neither such a certificate, nor a subsequent declaration of incompatibility under section 4 of the Act, renders legislation inoperable or unconstitutional, however odious its terms may be. If Parliament holds its ground, it wins, always.

My other defence against the charge of contrariness – the other reason why I am comfortable with our courts developing their own jurisprudence on Convention rights – is that our courts have an intimate understanding of the cultural and political norms within which they operate.

---

[32] Section 19 HRA:

> 19 Statements of compatibility
>
> (1) A Minister of the Crown in charge of a Bill in either House of Parliament must, before Second Reading of the Bill –
>> (a) make a statement to the effect that in his view the provisions of the Bill are compatible with the Convention rights ('a statement of compatibility'); or
>> (b) make a statement to the effect that although he is unable to make a statement of compatibility the government nevertheless wishes the House to proceed with the Bill.
>
> (2) The statement must be in writing and be published in such manner as the Minister making it considers appropriate.

The relationship between the political class and the judiciary is a subtle one; our judges are far from daft. Sometimes the political class is willing, praying, that the courts will act where they fear to tread. Thus, on the development of the law of privacy, Parliament has, albeit in an inchoate way, passed the parcel to the courts, and has been only too relieved that they have created an extensive body of law, and procedure, from the skeletons of Article 8 of the Convention and section 12 of the HRA.

When the Court of Appeal made its decision on anonymised evidence in criminal trials in *R* v. *Davis*[33] there were sighs of relief all round Whitehall. When the same decision was overturned by the law lords[34] there were groans in Whitehall, not least from me, since the decision meant that I had to introduce emergency legislation to fill the hole. But I could, as I said at the time, make no criticism of the law lords, as their argument was that the courts could not stretch the common law as we (the executive) had wanted – change had to be a matter for Parliament. Similar logic, of respect for Parliament, lay behind the Supreme Court's decision in *Mohamed, R* v. *Secretary of State for Foreign & Commonwealth Affairs*[35] to refuse to provide at common law 'closed material proceedings' in civil actions.

It is also worth repeating my point at the beginning of this lecture that where the decisions of Strasbourg have

---

[33] *R* v. *Davis (Appellant)*, [2006] EWCA Crim. 1155, [2006] 1 WLR 3130.
[34] *R* v. *Davis*, [2008] UKHL 36.
[35] *Mohamed, R (on the application of)* v. *Secretary of State for Foreign & Commonwealth Affairs*, [2010] EWCA Civ. 158.

caused problems – *Marper*[36] on DNA, *Hirst*[37] on prisoner voting rights, the earlier decisions in *Al-Khawaja*[38] – the British courts have endorsed Parliament's approach, and found it compatible with Convention rights.

So far I have been discussing the attitude of the British courts to Strasbourg and Convention rights, and the relationship of our courts to our parliament.

Let me now go on to deal with the relationship between our institutions and Strasbourg.

Baroness Hale wittily entitled her lecture, 'Argentoratum Locutum: Is the Supreme Court Supreme?' This was a play on the phrases which the late Lord Rodger had used when he was roundly complaining in *AF (No. 3)*[39] of the attitude of the Strasbourg Court. 'Argentoratum locutum, iudicium finitum' ('Strasbourg has spoken, the case is closed').

By all accounts, Strasbourg did not appreciate Lord Rodger's observation. It caused considerable sensitivity there, with Sir Nicolas Bratza, the now outgoing president of the Court, saying, 'Brilliantly Latinised as was the sentence ...

---

[36] *S. and Marper* v. *United Kingdom*, nos. 30562/04 and 30566/04, European Court of Human Rights, 4 December 2008.

[37] *Hirst* v. *United Kingdom (No. 2)*, (2004) 38 EHRR 40, and *Hirst* v. *United Kingdom (No. 2)*, no. 74025/01, European Court of Human Rights, 6 October 2005.

[38] *Al-Khawaja and Tahery* v. *United Kingdom*, no. 26766/05, [2011] ECHR 2127 (15 December 2011).

[39] *Secretary of State for the Home Department (Respondent)* v. *AF (Appellant) (FC) and another (Appellant) and one other action*, [2009] UKHL 28.

[this] is not the way which I or my fellows view the respective roles of the two courts'.[40]

The real complaint from Strasbourg, however, was that Lord Rodger's barb hit its target. That court has set itself up as Supreme Court for Europe, and one with an ever-expanding remit. It justifies this on the twin grounds that the Convention is a 'living instrument',[41] and that it is the duty of the Court to ensure that rights that they identify (in a growing list) should be applied in a uniform manner across the forty-seven member states of the Council of Europe.

If the Strasbourg Court has been irritated by remarks of jurists like Lord Rodger, it has displayed a degree of hauteur towards elected politicians, for example the Conservative MP and former Shadow Home Secretary, David Davis, and me. It's never been said in exactly these terms, but the implication of Strasbourg's attitude is that we are taking the view we do for crude and vulgar reasons of populism, and that it's the job of Strasbourg to protect the citizens of Europe from people like Mr Davis and me. The facts that we were elected (and, as it happens, for different parties) and that we have a direct democratic mandate having had a vote passed in the House of Commons by 234 to 22, are simply ignored.

It is, however, time for Strasbourg to note the breadth and weight of opinion here and, I suspect, in many other parts of Europe – and to pull back. Otherwise, Strasbourg will be the architect of its own demise.

[40] *Guardian*, 23 November 2011.
[41] *Tyrer* v. *United Kingdom*, no. 5856/72, European Court of Human Rights, 25 April 1978.

The fundamental difficulty with the lengths to which the Strasbourg Court has taken the 'living law' conception is that there is simply no authority whatever for it.

As I mentioned in my opening summary, the member states of the European Union have known in advance what they were signing up to. In the 1975 UK referendum on whether we should remain in the then European Communities (now Union), a major part of the argument was about whether we would lose sovereignty to Brussels and, if so, whether this was a price worth paying for the benefits of membership. That issue, of sovereignty and power, was at the heart of the argument twenty years ago over the Maastricht Treaty, over the proposed EU Constitution ten years ago, over Lisbon and every treaty change in between. People in this country can argue about the desirability of our membership of the EU, but no one can seriously claim that we were sold a pig in a poke, that the EU's key institutions, especially the Commission, and the Court in Luxembourg, have been acting in a way that no one anticipated and for which there is no agreed authority in the treaties and other parts of *acquis communautaire*.

But where has been the equivalent political, democratic engagement over the jurisdiction that Strasbourg has taken unto itself? Where are the treaty texts, where are the records of debates in the parliaments of the Council of Europe's member states? They don't exist. And what answer do we anticipate that the national parliaments of those member states might have given, if a draft text had been put before them saying that the Court in Strasbourg would have an ever-widening mandate to determine what shall constitute human rights, over which they should have the last word, where, once they had spoken, 'iudicium finitum'?

There is, for sure, authority in the treaties that the Convention, and its associated institutions, especially the Court, have the role of protecting basic human rights. These are those rights whose absence was a mark of the tyrannies that ruled so much of Europe for many decades – including the right to life, the right to a fair trial, the right to be neither tortured nor subject to cruel and degrading treatment. But, as Lord Hoffmann spelt out in a withering examination of Strasbourg's approach,[42] it is simply impossible to argue that this background justifies Strasbourg's detailed interpretation of the right of silence, the hearsay rule and – most preposterous of all – night flights at Heathrow airport, 'which sounds about as far from human rights as you could get'.[43]

Now it may be that as well as dismissing the arguments of common or garden politicians like David Davis and me, those who know better in Strasbourg also dismiss the views of jurists like Lord Hoffmann, Lord Irvine, the recently appointed Supreme Court Justice Jonathan Sumption[44] and many others, on the grounds that they are prejudiced. But what about the late Lord Bingham, whose human rights credentials were impeccable? In *Brown* v. *Stott*,[45] for instance, he said that '[i]n interpreting the Convention, as any other

---

[42] Lord Hoffmann, 'The Universality of Human Rights', Judicial Studies Board Annual Lecture, 19 March 2009.

[43] Ibid., 19.

[44] Jonathan Sumption, 'Judicial and Political Decision Making: The Uncertain Boundary', 35th F. A. Mann Lecture, 8 November 2011.

[45] [2003] 1 AC 681, 703.

treaty, it is generally to be assumed that the parties have included the terms which they wished to include and on which they were able to agree, omitting other terms which they did not wish to include or on which they were not able to agree.'

That's exactly the point we are all trying to make.

Which brings me to the margin of appreciation, the latitude which the Strasbourg Court believes that member states should be allowed in order to make their own decisions in their own political and cultural contexts about wider human rights beyond those basic ones whose protection was the purpose of the treaties.

One of the aims of the HRA was to ensure that the United Kingdom was able to enjoy a much greater margin of appreciation from Strasbourg than pre-incorporation because our courts would now themselves be adjudicating on issues before they went to Europe. Indeed, in the absence of any jurisdiction for the British courts over Convention rights, there wasn't much for Strasbourg to 'appreciate' one way or another, since there was silence where there should have been argument.

To some extent, this aim has been met. But there are still too many categories of case where Strasbourg succumbs to the temptation to adjudicate. Let us take the issue of DNA samples. There are certainly great arguments to be had over the rules that should be adopted for the taking, and retention, of such samples – but there were, in my view and that of many others, no grounds for Strasbourg effectively to decide to legislate over the heads of the British parliament, as it did in *Marper*.[46]

---

[46] *S. and Marper* v. *United Kingdom*, nos. 30562/04 and 30566/04, European Court of Human Rights, 4 December 2008.

Strasbourg has got into this difficulty because it believes that its extended definition of human rights should apply uniformly across all forty-seven member states. That would have been fine if there were warrant for this in the treaties and, crucially, if they had any means of ensuring that in practice there was a uniform enforcement of their judgments across those forty-seven member states. But there are not.

This brings me to the heart of the Strasbourg problem, exemplified by Lord Rodger's Latin epigram that the European Court of Human Rights has set itself up as a Supreme Court for Europe.

That would be fine, too, if this had been explicitly agreed, and if there was a 'democratic override' mechanism in place. In the areas of its competence, the European Court of Justice (ECJ) in Luxembourg is a kind of Supreme Court. But it has clear enforcement mechanisms, not least through the Commission, and, critically, there is provision for a degree of 'democratic override' in respect of its decisions. The rules may make such override difficult, but the Council of Ministers (formally the Council of the European Union) can change, and sometimes has changed, the relevant regulations or directives, by the same process (typically by qualified majority voting) which legislated for the original text.

No such democratic override, however, exists in respect of decisions made by Strasbourg. Once the Grand Chamber has pronounced, that's it, so far as its advocates are concerned.

This makes the Strasbourg Court unique.

There is not a national Supreme Court in the democratic world that I can identify for which there is not some form of override, however complex that may be. Where the powers of these courts are provided by written constitutions, as they almost always are, then override may be by way of a constitutional amendment, which normally requires a special majority. The United States has one of the most powerful, if not the most powerful, Supreme Courts in the world. Even there, the Court's decisions can be overturned by the will of the people. If the Supreme Court reaches a judgment with which Congress or particular states disagree, they can attempt to overturn the effect of the decision through an amendment to the constitution either through a 'national convention' assembled by two-thirds of state legislatures, or by a two-thirds vote in both houses of Congress, followed by ratification by four-fifths of state legislatures. This has been done on a number of occasions, most notably in the case of Congress's addition of the Fourteenth Amendment in order to give citizenship rights to all those born or naturalised in the United States, in order to 'overturn' the Supreme Court ruling in the case of *Dred Scott* v. *Sandford* in 1857.[47]

So long as the Strasbourg Court is confining itself to those basic rights for which it was established, then it can be argued – successfully argued, in my view – that there is consent for their decisions, and they should not be ignored or gainsaid. If, for example, the Strasbourg Court decides that it is unsafe to deport, say, a terrorist suspect, notwithstanding assurances about their treatment, then no home or interior minister is going to ignore that decision, nor should they, however irritating it may be. That has been the

---

[47] *Dred Scott* v. *Sandford*, (1857) 60 US 393.

consistent approach of all British Home Secretaries, me included, so far as I am aware. Michael Howard, hardly an enthusiast for the Convention, observed the Court's decision in *Chahal*; other holders of that office have done similarly before and since; and in every case our parliament has accepted this, too.

But, as we all know, the Court has not confined itself to these basic rights. It has ranged much wider – into those areas highlighted by Lord Hoffmann and others, and into prisoner voting rights. Testament to this fact is the backlog of cases awaiting judgment by the Court, which at present numbers 138,000.[48] As Professor Timothy Endicott, Dean of the Faculty of Law at Oxford, has commented, 'if we take away [a prisoner's] right to vote then I don't think that's an abuse of them as a human being any more than it's an abuse of them as a human being to take away their freedom of movement'.[49]

And here's the problem that the Strasbourg Court has failed to think through and that will lead to its demise if it continues on this course.

What happens next if, faced with the decisions we have to make on prisoner voting rights, our democratically elected representatives say, quite legitimately, 'Sorry, we don't agree, and we shall not implement your judgements'?

---

[48] 'UK risks undermining human rights legislation, Europe's top judge warns', *Guardian*, 21 October 2012.

[49] 'A Shift in the Attitude of European Courts towards Human Rights Law? An Interview with Prof. Timothy Endicott, Dean of the Faculty of Law, Oxford University', *Harvard Human Rights Journal*, 1 May 2012.

That's what has happened for the last seven years, and the situation is likely to continue. On the last occasion there was a vote on the matter in the House of Commons, there was a clear majority (of 212) against changing the law,[50] and on top of this every opinion poll conducted on this issue to date shows similarly strong support by the public for the UK government's current position.

When the Strasbourg Court reviewed its approach in the more recent decision of *Scoppola* v. *Italy (No. 3)*[51] it noted this vote (it had been part of the case advanced by our own Attorney General, Dominic Grieve QC) but then ignored it.

Mention the absence of any democratic override for the Court's decisions, and one is met with condescension and glazed eyes.

But the issue will not, indeed, cannot, go away – and it's time for Strasbourg to heed, not ignore, all the warnings conveyed to it, now not just by politicians but by jurists as well.

There's an irony here, too. In its discussion of the general principles to inform its judgment, the Court, in *Scoppola*, said that 'any conditions [to restrict prisoner's right to vote] must not thwart the free expression of the people in the choice of legislature', and quoted Article 3 of Protocol 1 in their support.[52] But what if the 'free expression of the will of the people' includes their will that convicted prisoners should not vote? There is absolutely no doubt that this is the will of

---

[50] Hansard, 10 February 2011.
[51] *Scoppola* v. *Italy (No. 3)*, no. 126/05, [2012] ECHR 868, 22 May 2012.
[52] Ibid., at para. 84.

the British people on this issue – so what is the Court's attitude to them? Ignore that will, fail to meet the expectations of the self-same Article 3 of Protocol 1?

A conflict between Strasbourg's ever-widening juris-diction, and the will of the people of member states was bound to occur at some stage. It's incidental that it's happened over prisoner voting rights, and the responsibility for resolving it lies squarely with the Court, not the UK parliament.

There are those who say that the UK parliament will have to concede; we have no choice. Sir Nicolas has lectured us, saying that, 'I do think that it's seen as damaging that a country as important as the UK has not complied with a court judgment yet.' I'm afraid that I see it as damaging that this court should seek to tell my constituents what to think, when they have had no opportunity to agree or to decline that invitation. These are 'there be dragons' arguments, and I am afraid that I find them wholly unconvincing. The more subtle argument is that we would be breaching the rule of law. But the rule of law has to be a two-way street in a democracy; it has to be founded on some democratic authority, and it is that which is lacking here. In any event, as Lord Irvine draws attention to in his lecture, 'implementation action [in respect of ECtHR judgments] is consequently a matter for political decision within the [Council of Europe] and is not of a *judicial* political character'.[53]

I have never argued that the United Kingdom should leave the Convention, and I do not do so here. For all its many

---

[53] Lord Irvine of Lairg- *A British Interpretation of Convention Rights* (14 December 2011, UCL Judicial Institute).

frustrations I believe that the Convention, and its application by the Court, has overall been a force for good. But institutions can tip over, or decay, if they overreach themselves. 'Pride *goeth* before destruction, and an haughty spirit before a fall',[54] is the injunction of Proverbs, and one which the Strasbourg Court needs better to heed.

It is Strasbourg which will be the loser if it continues its present approach. Human rights in the United Kingdom will in any event continue to be protected so long as the Human Rights Act remains in force; and it's my prediction that it will, come what may.

---

[54] Proverbs 16:18.

3

Judicial appointments

The president of Egypt, Mohamed Morsi, Sir Brian Leveson, and women bishops – all provoking headlines in late November 2012 as I wrote the lecture on which this final chapter is based – do not at first blush have much to connect them. But in different ways they provide a reminder of the significance of the apparently prosaic theme of this final chapter, judicial appointments.

President Morsi's decree preventing the judiciary from reviewing his decisions, and the intense controversy that has followed in its wake, underlines how crucial to a properly functioning state is the relationship between its executive and its judiciary.

Lord Justice Leveson's inquiry into the press is yet another testament to the very high standing in which the British judiciary is held, and to the regularity with which ministers and Parliament send for a judge to solve an apparently intractable problem.

And the furore over the Church of England's failure to agree to the introduction of women bishops should alert us all to the impatience now felt about the tardy pace at which many of our institutions, public and private, are moving towards achieving serious equality of gender – and, I would add, ethnicity – in our society.

In this lecture I shall

- first, review the current system for making judicial appointments;
- second, reflect on the proper role, if any, of politicians in these appointments; and
- third, consider what more should be done to speed progress towards a judiciary which at every level more accurately reflects the make-up of the society it serves.

The appointment of judges – by whom, according to what standards and process, and with what outcome – is of critical importance. To maintain a judiciary that is independent, which makes good decisions, and in whom the public can continue to have confidence, we need to appoint the most meritorious candidates and secure a judiciary that is as reflective as possible of the society it is serving.

And we need to get it right first time, every time, because, once appointed to a full-time salaried position, judges may not be removed from office other than in the most extreme of circumstances.[1]

Appointments to the judiciary were, until the passing of the 2005 Constitutional Reform Act, the responsibility of the Lord Chancellor. He signed off all appointments. He

---

[1] Judges of the High Court and above hold office during good behaviour, subject to a power of removal by Her Majesty on an Address presented to Her by both Houses of Parliament (Senior Courts Act 1981, s. 11(3)). Judges below High Court level hold office during good behaviour, subject to a power of removal by the Lord Chancellor with the concurrence of the Lord Chief Justice.

made senior appointments himself, having consulted senior members of the judiciary.

From the mid-1990s this system was much reviewed and formalised. Appointments were opened up to applications rather than being made on an invitation-only basis, job descriptions and assessment centres began to appear, and the process was made subject to independent audit and oversight. But all this was non-statutory. However fair the system was in fact, it continued to lack that essential ingredient of appearing to be fair as well.

As it happens the system did work satisfactorily in many ways. For the previous three or four decades, holders of the office of Lord Chancellor made judicial appointments scrupulously, and without reference to politically partisan considerations.

However, the position of the old-style Lord Chancellor was plainly time-expired. In a very British way, it had remained entirely at odds with any Montesquieu-style notion of the separation of powers. The Lord Chancellor was the holy trinity all by himself – senior cabinet minister, Speaker of the House of Lords, and head of the judiciary.

In the modern climate, with the Lord Chancellor and his department more and more involved in the general work of government, this role, and this system for making judicial appointments, couldn't last.

It came to an end with the Constitutional Reform Act 2005.

For judicial appointments, the aim was to devise a system that protected the proper independence of the judiciary from political interference or influence, while reflecting the legitimate interest of the executive and Parliament in the quality of justice, the efficiency and effectiveness of the court system, and in the wider role of our senior courts, especially the new UK Supreme Court.

There was also the hope that it would deal with the stubborn inability of the previous system to make appointments that reflected diversity. The assumption regarding diversity – naïve, as it turned out – was that if we changed the process, we would change the outcome.

The CRA provided for the establishment of an independent Judicial Appointments Commission (JAC).

The JAC was made responsible for operating the appointments process and making recommendations to the Lord Chancellor for all but the most senior appointments. For these very senior appointments (to the Court of Appeal, and the offices of Head of Division, Lord Chief Justice, and the president, deputy president and members of the UK Supreme Court), separate provision was made for recommendations to be made to the Lord Chancellor by specially constituted selection panels.

For each appointment, the JAC, or the specially constituted selection panel, was required to make one recommendation to the Lord Chancellor.

On being presented with a recommendation the Lord Chancellor then had, in theory, a range of options. He could:

- accept the recommendation;
- reject it, on the grounds that the person is unsuitable for the office; or

- ask for it to be reconsidered on the grounds either that there is not enough evidence that the person is suitable, or that there is evidence that the person is not the best candidate on merit.[2]

In practice, as I found out through painful experience, there were a number of problems with this set-up.

For lower-level appointments, below the High Court, the role of the Lord Chancellor became simply that of a signature-writing machine. It was, frankly, absurd, bordering on the risible. With the increase in the number of people at the Bar and the limits on the amount of information that the JAC could put forward and that I could realistically absorb, it was impossible for me to make well-informed judgements about whether the JAC had got their decision-making right. I doubt whether under previous arrangements the Lord Chancellor ever really had a meaningful role in relation to these appointments.

The Crime and Courts Bill, which is before the House of Lords as I write this chapter, proposes transferring this role to the Lord Chief Justice, or the Senior President of Tribunals, as appropriate. This is eminently sensible.

But Parliament has accepted, and restated, that there continues to be a role for the Lord Chancellor in relation to the most senior appointments. The question is, what precisely should that role be?

---

[2] Ss. 29 and 30 of the Constitutional Reform Act, in respect of the UK Supreme Court; ss. 73 and 74 in respect of the Lord Chief Justice and Heads of Division; ss. 75E and 75F in respect of the Senior President of Tribunals; and ss. 82 and 83 in respect of Court of Appeal appointments.

I accept that the role of the Lord Chancellor in relation to High Court and Court of Appeal appointments should be limited. But for the two groups of our most senior judges, and for different reasons, in my view the Lord Chancellor should have a greater role than is provided for by the Constitutional Reform Act, or than is likely to be provided for by the current Crime and Courts Bill.

The two groups of judges I am talking about are, first, the most senior members of the Court of Appeal – that is, the Heads of Division and Lord Chief Justice – and, second, the members of the UK Supreme Court. The conclusion is the same, but the arguments are different.

Taking the first group first, the Lord Chief Justice is by law the head of the judiciary. This post, and those of his immediate colleagues, the Heads of Division, require not only high skills as jurists, but also considerable leadership and administrative expertise, and the ability to work effectively with the Ministry of Justice, the Courts Service and other organs of government.

Since the Lord Chancellor has responsibility to Parliament for these services, and crucially for the vote of their money, the Lord Chancellor has an entirely legitimate interest in the qualities of those who fill these posts.

There is no equivalent executive and administrative responsibility for the Supreme Court's president and its members. They sit above the structure. So the case I make is a different one.

Notwithstanding the elegance of section 4 of the Human Rights Act, which prevents our senior courts from overruling primary legislation made by Parliament, the UK Supreme Court can, as it has done, declare parliament-made legislation incompatible with the ECHR. In practice it is very difficult, though lawful, for a minister to ignore such a declaration.

The court has defined its discretion under the HRA role quite narrowly (as I discussed at some length in Chapter 2), making decisions on key issues such as DNA, anonymised evidence in criminal trials and closed material proceedings in a way which, as it happens, has deferred to Parliament's sovereignty.[3] Nonetheless, the Supreme Court's role is wide, and its judgments inevitably have an impact on our politics and our lives. However much the individual members are themselves detached from party politics, who they are – their perspective, their life experience, their approach – matters, and is evident from their judgments, too.

All of this is already recognised, in principle at least, by the Constitutional Reform Act, which provides that these two groups of very senior appointments should not be made by the normal Judicial Appointments Commission process.

The reality of a connection between the senior judiciary and the executive is also recognised in almost every other jurisdiction. By far the most usual approach elsewhere in the world, including in well-functioning common-law jurisdictions, is for the relevant minister to be recommended three to five names, and for that minister then to be able to

---

[3] See *R (GC and C)* v. *Commissioner of Police for the Metropolis*, [2011] UKSC 21; *R* v. *Davis*, [2008] UKHL 36, *Mohamed, R (on the application of)* v. *Secretary of State for Foreign & Commonwealth Affairs*, [2010] EWCA Civ. 158.

choose from among these nominees. In the United Kingdom we are very unusual in insisting that the minister receives one name alone. This is explicable only in the context of where we have come from: the untrammelled discretion of the Lord Chancellor until the mid 1990s, the non-statutory nature of the pre-2005 arrangements, the opaque decision-making process and the mounting criticism of it.

But these literally peculiar arrangements for these very senior appointments, intended to create a partnership approach between the judiciary and the Lord Chancellor in recognition of the requirements of the offices in question, have proved to be unsatisfactory.

Both the detailed wording[4] and the expectation in practice make it very difficult for the Lord Chancellor to exercise even his limited powers to reject or request a reconsideration of a recommendation. As is a matter of record in the press, there was one occasion when, as Lord Chancellor, I sought to use these powers.

Since I have always observed the confidentiality necessary for the consideration of such appointments I am not here going to go into any detail. I hope, however, that it will be accepted that I would not have sought to exercise these powers unless I had believed that I had grounds within the Act for doing so. I did – good grounds, as many can now see. I went to considerable lengths to ensure that my actions could

---

[4] Ss. 29–31 of the Constitutional Reform Act, in respect of the UK Supreme Court; ss. 73–75 in respect of Lord Chief Justice and Heads of Division; ss. 75E–75G in respect of the Senior President of Tribunals; and ss. 82–84 in respect of Court of Appeal appointments.

not be construed, which they were not remotely, as party political. In the event, the matter was not seen through to a conclusion. Partisans to the appointment – not anyone directly involved in the process – leaked extensive detail to the press; an election was looming; I confirmed the appointment.

Parliament's intention cannot in practice happen with the current text of the CRA. It hasn't worked. In solving one problem (too much executive power) we went too far the other way, missing the solution used by almost every other jurisdiction.

The government's Crime and Courts Bill will improve matters somewhat. It will allow the Lord Chancellor to become involved before the selection panel has reached a conclusion, but what is proposed does not, in my view, go far enough.

This bill looks set to provide that the Lord Chancellor should, in addition to his powers to accept, reject or request a reconsideration, be consulted prior to the start of the selection process for appointments at Court of Appeal level and above.

The bill also remedies the position we created in the Constitutional Reform Act by which the president of the Supreme Court was able, effectively, to appoint not only new members of the court, but his successor as president. This would not be acceptable anywhere else these days. I am pleased that different arrangements are being proposed.

The bill in its original form put forward by Ken Clarke provided for the Lord Chancellor to sit on the selection panels for the offices of Lord Chief Justice and president of the UK Supreme Court. However, it appears that the new Lord Chancellor, Chris Grayling, does not wish to press ahead with this provision. I regret this. While the current Lord Chancellor might not wish to avail himself of this opportunity, it should in my view be made available for his successors – and not just for these two appointments, but for Heads of Division and UK Supreme Court appointments as well.

I want to turn now to diversity.

Like many others before me, I start by setting out why diversity is something with which we should be concerned.

Judges must have distinctive qualifications and experience. For this reason, they cannot immediately reflect the demography of the country as a whole, any more than can doctors, accountants or engineers. But if you want the best possible judiciary, you have to work hard to make it as reflective as possible of the society it serves – a society that is divided half male and half female, where more than one in ten are black or Asian, a significant minority are gay, lesbian or bisexual,[5] 15 per cent are disabled,[6] and 93 per cent are educated at state schools.[7]

This is for three reasons.

First, judges wield a great deal of power. From a democratic point of view, the bench needs to look as much as possible like the society it is serving, to avoid the

---

[5] A 2005 survey by HM Treasury and the Department of Trade and Industry came up with an estimate of around 6 per cent. The first ONS Household Survey to ask a question on sexuality in 2010 came up with a figure of 1.5 per cent.

[6] Office for Disability Issues, Family Resources Survey 2010/2011, figure for working-age adults.

[7] '"Embers from the Ashes"? The Experience of Being an Assisted Place Holder', Sutton Trust, May 2009.

concentration of power in the hands of a small section of society, and to promote public confidence in its individual decisions and its legitimacy as an institution. To paraphrase Bill Clinton, we need a judiciary that 'looks like Britain rather than looking like us'.[8]

Second, diversity means that a range of perspectives, life experiences and backgrounds can be brought to bear both within an institution and on decision-making itself. More diverse courts are better equipped to carry out the role of adjudicating than courts that are not diverse.

And, third, if we accept the assumption that talent is randomly and widely distributed among the population rather than being concentrated in particular groups of people, then the under-representation of well-qualified women, black and Asian judges, gay and lesbian judges, disabled judges, suggests that we are missing out on the best. Either they are not applying, or they are not coming through the process.

These are the elements of the 'business case' for diversity. But there is a fourth important argument here. It is that equality matters as a matter of principle. As the House of Lords Select Committee said in its report on these matters earlier this year, 'Justice, fairness and equality are central values in the law which should be reflected in the composition of the judiciary itself.'[9]

Looking across society, progress towards a more equal and fairer society has been patchy.

---

[8] Bill Clinton spoke about the US judiciary looking 'like America'.
[9] House of Lords Select Committee on the Constitution, Judicial Appointments, 28 March 2012.

In some ways there were more opportunities for someone from my background to get into a decent set of chambers in the Inner Temple back in the 1970s than there are today. I benefited from a scholarship to board at a direct grant school; I was given a full student grant for my three years as an undergraduate, and a full grant for my year at Bar School; and I then won a scholarship – those do still exist – to fund my pupillage. In some respects the legal profession and society as a whole are no less elitist now than they were then.[10] On income equality we have made little progress.[11]

But is it better now than when I first came to the Bar forty years ago, to be born a woman in this country? Yes. Is it better now than then to be born black or Asian? Yes. Gay or lesbian? Undoubtedly yes.

As I discuss in my autobiography, *Last Man Standing*, some of my proudest achievements from my thirteen years in government relate to this fundamental issue of equality. Establishing the judicial inquiry under Sir William

---

[10] The Sutton Trust report, 'The Educational Backgrounds of Leading Lawyers, Journalists, Vice Chancellors, Politicians, Medics and Chief Executives', March 2009, notes that 'the young partners of today are almost as likely to have been educated in private schools (71 per cent) as the older partners of twenty years ago (73 per cent). So while the law firms did appear to open up to a generation of partners educated in state secondary schools in the 1960s (predominantly grammar schools), this does not look to be a lasting change, and more recent recruitment appears to have resulted in a growth in the representation of those from the fee-paying sector.'

[11] The Gini coefficient measure of overall income inequality in the United Kingdom is now higher than at any previous time in the last thirty years – see www.poverty.org.uk.

Macpherson, a retired High Court judge, into the death of Stephen Lawrence and then ensuring that its findings were implemented remain among my proudest achievements, resulting eventually, nearly nineteen years after Stephen's murder, in the conviction of two of his killers. It has also led to a seminal change in the place of black and Asian people in our society. The number of black and Asian police officers has risen markedly. The face of many of our institutions has changed. There has been a deep-seated cultural change away from the pernicious, sniggering racism of the 1970s, 80s and 90s towards a more mature, tolerant, fair society.

I was also determined, as Home Secretary, to do something about the punitive legislation and public attitudes surrounding homosexuality. The equalisation of the age of consent for gay sex was eventually carried, using the Parliament Acts to override the Lords' opposition, in November 2000. Section 28 of the Local Government Act 1988 banning local authorities from 'intentionally promot[ing] homosexuality', was repealed in 2003, also after repeated blocking in the Lords. None of the absurd predictions about the erosion of society that would occur if we treated gay and lesbian people equally and with respect came to pass. Indeed, the reverse is the case, and we have a fairer society, more at ease with itself.

Four reasons, then, why diversity within the judiciary is important: legitimacy, a breadth of perspectives, ensuring that we find the best talent, and finally straightforward justice and fairness.

There has been progress since this issue first became a concern, twenty years, four Lord Chief Justices, and five Lord Chancellors ago.

- In 1992, 5 per cent of recorders, 5 per cent of circuit judges, 5 per cent of recorders and 10 per cent of assistant recorders were women and there were believed to be three black or Asian judges, seven recorders and seven assistant recorders.
- By 1998, just over 10 per cent of the 3,174 courts-based judges in post were women, and 1.6 per cent black or Asian.
- The equivalent figures in 2012 are that well over 22 per cent of judges are now women, and 4.2 per cent are black or Asian.

The JAC is keen to emphasise the progress achieved since its establishment. I have no wish to cavil, and I commend the vigour with which the newly constituted JAC is approaching this challenge. It can justifiably point to improvements. Comparing the six years (2000–6) immediately preceding the JAC to the six since, the proportion of High Court appointments who are women has risen from 12.7 per cent to 19.7 per cent, and district judges (magistrates' courts) from 29.1 per cent to 43.1 per cent, with notable improvements for the part-time fee-paid posts too. Black and minority ethnic (BME) appointments have also shifted to some extent – in the High Court from 1.8 per cent to 3.3 per cent, and among deputy district judges too.

That said, progress has been frustratingly slow, from a low base. It is twenty years since the then Lord Chief Justice, the late Lord Taylor, said,

> The present imbalance between male and female, white and black, in the judiciary, is obvious . . . I have no doubt that the balance will be redressed in the next few years.[12]

---

[12] Lord Taylor of Gosforth, 'The Judiciary in the Nineties', The Dimbleby Lecture, 1992.

In the same year, Lord Mackay of Clashfern, then Lord Chancellor, commissioned the first[13] of what was to become a slew of reports and inquiries into the issue.

For anyone who has been keeping half an eye on progress since then, Lord Taylor's prediction now seems a tad optimistic. The balance was not redressed within a few years; twenty years on, it has not been redressed; and few believe that it might be within the next few years. This is especially the case at the most senior levels of the judiciary, where we had to wait until 1998 for Elizabeth Butler-Sloss to be appointed the first woman to the Court of Appeal, and until 2004 for Linda Dobbs to be appointed the first ethnic minority High Court judge.[14]

The stark difference between the senior and lower levels of the judiciary is captured by the phrase, the 'prestige effect'.

Where women and minorities have gained appointment to the judiciary, it is primarily at lower levels. For women, there is the additional 'caring effect': women are most likely to attain judicial office in the 'caring' tribunals (Mental Health, Special Educational Needs, Family Health and so on), and in

---

[13] Lesley Holland and Lynne Spencer, *Without Prejudice? Sex Equality at the Bar and in the Judiciary* (London: Bar Council).

[14] Brenda, now Baroness, Hale was in 1993 the first academic appointed to the High Court. In 1994 solicitors first appeared as advocates, and in 1997 Arthur Marriott and Lawrence Collins were the first two solicitors to be appointed QCs. Baroness Hale was appointed the first – and still the only – female law lord in 2004. Sir Michael Sachs was the first solicitor to be appointed to the High Court in 1993. In 2000 Lawrence Collins became the first solicitor appointed to the High Court bench direct from private practice and then, in 2007, the first former solicitor to be appointed to the Court of Appeal.

the Family Division. Women have significantly lower representation in either Chancery or the Queen's Bench Division.

For black and Asian candidates, the increases at circuit
judge, district judge and recorder level have been disappointing.
The issues here are complex. I have heard, anecdotally but from
very different sources, that black and Asian lawyers who have
reached the pinnacle of their profession are often not inclined
to put themselves forward for judicial office. On the other hand,
the JAC's statistics show that black and Asian candidates are
applying in significantly higher numbers post-JAC than pre-
JAC. But they are not getting through the process in anything
like those numbers. There's a puzzle to be solved here.

So what do we do, if we believe as I do that while
welcoming the shifts which have taken place, a lot more needs
to be done?

The Supreme Court justice Jonathan Sumption
recently gave an entertaining and thought-provoking lecture
about judicial diversity.[15] 'We need, as a society,' he said,
'to have an honest public debate about the hitherto unmen-
tionable subject of positive discrimination.'

I commend his frankness. But I dispute his conten-
tion that,

> Few constituencies would be more seriously affected by
> the introduction of diversity as a criterion for selecting
> judges than women and ethnic minorities. Positive
> discrimination is patronising.

[15] Lord Sumption, 'Home Truths about Judicial Diversity', Bar Council
Law Reform Lecture, 15 November 2012, available at www.supremecourt.
gov.uk/docs/speech-121115-lord-sumption.pdf.

And his arguments that,

> There are two reasons why making diversity a criterion for appointment would adversely affect the quality of appointments. The first one is self-evident. If you dilute the principle of selecting only the most talented candidates by introducing criteria other than individual merit, you will by definition end up with a bench on which there are fewer outstanding people. But there is a more serious problem even than that. It is the impact that the change would have on applications.

Lord Sumption's conclusion is (and here I paraphrase, but not much) that we'll just have to wait for progress towards a more diverse judiciary, especially at the top.

There is an irony here as Lord Sumption seeks to defend the traditional forms of appointment to the higher judiciary, since he is a recent and controversial example of someone being appointed by a non-traditional route.

My fundamental objection to this line of argument is that it wrong-headedly pits merit and diversity against each other, implying that they must be mutually exclusive. I simply dispute the view that if you do something positive to help women and people from ethnic minorities to get on, that means that merit must suffer. Quite the reverse is true. If we want the best, we must look widely, not just within one narrow group, to find it. To quote Lord Neuberger, from the evidence he gave recently to the House of Lords Constitution Committee,

> If ... women are not less good judges than men, why are 80 per cent or 90 per cent of judges male? It suggests,

purely on a statistical basis, that we do not have the best people because there must be some women out there who are better than the less good men who are judges.[16]

Allow me, for a moment, a diversion. I want to talk about what has happened with members of parliament.

When I entered the House of Commons in 1979 there were just nineteen female MPs – 3 per cent of the total, and down on the previous election, which had returned twenty-seven women. The numbers did not move much in the following decade.[17] Mrs Thatcher had not favoured special measures for women – her view was that politics (like the Ritz) was open to all and talent would out.

In the run-up to the 1997 general election, the Labour Party used all-women shortlists to select candidates in half of all winnable seats. The policy was highly controversial. Some local Labour parties were very upset. Many people – or, to be more precise, many men – were fearful that the quality of candidates would fall, saying places would go to (and this is a direct quote) 'people who have no merit but who happen to wear a skirt'. In 1995, two men, supported by the Equal Opportunities Commission, took the party to court, successfully claiming sex discrimination.[18]

---

[16] Evidence to the House of Lords Constitution Committee, Q251, 12 October 2011.

[17] In the 1983, 1987 and 1992 elections, twenty-three, forty-one and sixty women respectively were returned.

[18] *Jepson and Dyas-Elliott* v. *The Labour Party and others*, [1996] IRLR 116 IT.

But the candidates who had already been selected by all-women shortlists were not required to re-stand for nomination. After the 2001 election the Labour government introduced the Sex Discrimination (Election Candidates) Act 2002 to enable them to continue to use discrimination in the selection of candidates.

A total of 101 Labour women MPs were elected in 1997, doubling the number of women MPs overnight. David Cameron's 'Priority-' or 'A-list' announced in 2005 was designed to achieve a similar aim, though by slightly different means.

The outcome is that 143 women MPs – 22 per cent of the total – were returned in 2010, seven times the number when I became an MP. The Labour party had managed to increase its proportion of women MPs to 34 per cent, the Conservatives were up at 15 per cent. The proportion of black and Asian MPs rose to 4.2 per cent, made up of 16 Labour MPs and 11 Conservatives. For the first time in my parliamentary career, the Commons is beginning to look more like the society it represents.

Despite the insults about skirts, and the snide comments about those women who 'had only managed it' because of the 'assisted places scheme', it is my observation that the quality of the women MPs on both sides of the House is higher than the quality of the men, while at the same time the quality of the most recent intake of male MPs is significantly better than it was thirty years ago. And this is what one should expect if one believes that talent is not concentrated in one small pocket of the population. Jonathan Sumption's assertion that the consequence of measures of positive discrimination is that 'by definition' you end up with 'fewer outstanding people' has no foundation in fact.

Two MPs have taken maternity leave since the 2010 election and another is pregnant. A Tory MP of my acquaintance is away on paternity leave. This reflects the realities of how life is lived. The sky has not fallen in.

This rapid, game-changing progress would not have been made without radical and controversial change in the whole mechanism of selection.

Something similar is happening where quotas have been introduced in the business world. In Norway, the government has mandated that there should be at least 40 per cent representation of each gender on the boards of publicly quoted companies since January 2008. As Dr Ruth Sealy and Professor Susan Vinnicombe of Cranfield University report,

> There is still debate as to whether it has been good or indifferent to businesses themselves. But there is no evidence of businesses imploding and new academic evidence emerging suggests that the new female board members are more qualified than their male counterparts; and are making significant contributions.

The Civil Service has managed to increase diversity at all levels without anyone suggesting that the quality of its work has declined.[19]

---

[19] In March 2012, nine (23 per cent) of the thirty-nine permanent secretaries across the Civil Service were women. House of Commons Library Standard Note, 'Women in Public Life, the Professions and the Boardroom', SN/SG/5170, 9 March 2012.

I know that many lawyers, many judges, possibly most of those who read this chapter, will throw your hands in the air and say, how can you compare us with MPs, civil servants, business people. We are different.

I am not so sure about this difference. MPs, after all, are lawmakers.

Then the lawyers will say, but it is set out in statute that we are different. We appoint, by statute, 'solely on merit'. It is possible, for us, because we are different, to distinguish at a very fine level between an extremely good candidate and an even more extremely good candidate. So we can always find the person with the most merit. And to appoint anyone other than that person would mean not getting the most meritorious candidate. Therefore women-only shortlists or any other kind of positive discrimination would lead to less meritorious candidates being appointed.

I am not so sure about this either.

Merit is an empty vessel which needs careful filling. It can all too easily mean 'people like us'. Unintentional selection bias – as Professor Hazel Genn, a former JAC Commissioner, argues – can lead to the over-valuation of certain familiar traits and ways of presenting, and the under-valuation of the unfamiliar.

Appointing 'on merit' does not necessarily result in the most meritorious, or best, candidates being appointed. That could be because the best candidates aren't applying, or because merit has been wrongly defined, or because there is something else going wrong in the process.

I am also far from convinced that no two candidates are ever of equal merit – that it is always possible to rank candidates one ahead of the other in what my predecessor Charlie Falconer has referred to as a top ten, or league table of brilliance sort of way.[20] This speaks to an unrealistic, illusory concept of merit, in my view. In reality, in both large exercises and small, and especially at the very highest levels, there are often situations where two or several candidates are equally meritorious. I know from my experience in the appointments processes for very senior roles – permanent secretaries, ambassadors, chief inspectors of prisons, probation, constabulary – that one is often faced with trying to make very fine distinctions between three or four very able candidates, all of whom would do an excellent job. Or, sometimes, with trying to predict which of three or four candidates would do the least worst job.

Given the desirability of improving the diversity of our judiciary I am wholly in favour, in these circumstances, of appointing a candidate who comes from an under-represented group over one who does not – to be clear, a woman over an equally meritorious man, or a black candidate over an equally meritorious white candidate.

The tipping-point provisions in the current draft of the Crime and Courts Bill, which make it clear that acting in such a way would be lawful, notwithstanding the Constitutional Reform Act's 'solely on merit' stipulation, are important. I would like to see them used assertively. But if the JAC and those on selection panels cling to the top-ten approach, I fear that this change will, as Jonathan Sumption has said, have limited effect.

---

[20] Evidence to House of Lords Constitution Committee, Q152, 12 October 2011.

There is much else that we can and should do in pursuit of a more diverse judiciary, short of positive discrimination – as Baroness Neuberger set out in her excellent 2010 Report, commissioned by me when I was Lord Chancellor.[21]

The legal profession must play its part; more must be done to encourage the widest possible range of people to apply to join the judiciary; we must continue to improve the appointments process; and we need to tackle some aspects of the judicial culture.

Progress on diversity in the judiciary is, for obvious reasons, dependent on progress on diversity in the legal profession.

The legal profession is working to attract and retain a more diverse group of lawyers, and making some progress. It is, paradoxically, not being helped at the front end by the huge expansion in lawyers in training. 1,600 students a year now take the Bar Professional Training Course at British law schools. That is more than three times the number of pupillages available at barristers' chambers. As Michael Todd, chairman of the Bar Council, has observed, 'This [oversupply] will do nothing to help the diversity and social mobility vital to ensuring our profession represents the society it serves.' It allows law firms and chambers to be wasteful of talent in unusual places, and to filter candidates according to narrowly defined criteria.

But it is retention and promotion rates that really need attention. Lord Neuberger said recently,

---

[21] Report of the Advisory Panel on Judicial Diversity, February 2010.

The proportion of women and ethnic minorities [in the legal profession] decreases as one goes up the ladder, and the fact that the higher up the ladder one goes, the more one is looking at historic intakes, is nothing like a complete explanation.[22]

Other explanations are the difficulties of balancing a successful legal career with family responsibilities (many previous high-fliers find themselves on the 'mummy track' as opposed to the 'partner track' when they return to work after having children), the promotion of 'people like us', and, frankly, overtly discriminatory views and behaviours. *Legal Week*'s most recent Big Question survey found that 58 per cent of 169 partners in the commercial legal sector witnessed blatant sexism on a fairly regular basis.[23]

When I was Lord Chancellor, one of my happy functions was to preside over the annual Silk ceremony. I used to make a mental note of the women and people from ethnic minorities there and for the three years I was there the numbers stayed depressingly static. They have remained static since then as well.[24]

We also need to encourage the widest possible group of talented people, from all walks of life and all backgrounds, to apply to become judges: women, black and Asian people,

---

[22] Lord Neuberger, 'Reforming Legal Education', Lord Upjohn Lecture, Association of Law Teachers, 15 November 2012.

[23] *Legal Week*'s Big Question survey, 26 October 2012.

[24] The proportion of women silks increased from 9 per cent to 12 per cent between 2006 and 2011, and the proportion of black and Asian silks from 4 per cent to 5 per cent over the same period.

lesbians and gay men, the disabled, solicitors, legal executives, government lawyers, academics, those of different religions and of none, those from a working-class background. As noted by a delegate to the International Summit on Judicial Diversity held in London in 2005, 'you should not be looking for unusual talent, but looking for talent in unusual places'.

One irony of the creation of the JAC and the quite deliberate move away from the 'tap on the shoulder' is that Lord Chancellors who wanted to take bold action to improve diversity, by spotting and appointing particular talented candidates, were no longer able to do so. This was the price we paid for moving to a fairer and more transparent system. But we were so eager to remove all trace of the 'tap on the shoulder' that we went too far the other way. While we may not be able to guarantee to anyone that they will get through the appointments process, there is nothing wrong with encouraging groups of people in general, and talented individuals in particular. Baroness Neuberger called it the 'pat on the back' rather than the 'tap on the shoulder'. In other walks of life it is called mentoring. There is still not enough of this going on: it can make an enormous difference to individuals who would otherwise have thought that the judiciary was not for them.

We need to keep looking at the selection process. The JAC model of an independent appointments commission is, at a macro level, the right one. But I am not persuaded that the process cannot be improved. As one example, honest and sensitive feedback provided person-to-person to talented applicants who just miss out would do something to improve the current situation in which excellent candidates from under-represented groups are persuaded to apply, do not succeed and then never reapply.

And we need to look at the judicial culture and terms and conditions. Pre-appointment training, and appraisal for serving judges, are important recommendations from Baroness Neuberger's report where progress has been disappointing.

I am, though, delighted that the Crime and Courts Bill will open the statutory door to more flexible working patterns in our highest courts, by expressing the judicial headcount ceiling for the UK Supreme Court, the Court of Appeal and the High Court in terms of full-time equivalents rather than individual office-holders. This change, if backed up with practical action and the willingness to consider doing some things differently, will widen considerably the group of people who see a judicial career as something that could be for them, and make it possible for the judiciary to benefit from the contribution of men and women with childcare or elder-care responsibilities who otherwise could not have served.

Finally, I am particularly pleased that effort is being put into statistics and evaluation. This whole discussion has been hampered by a frustrating absence of either decent data or meaningful evaluation of what works. It is hard to pinpoint how much of what progress there has been has been down to any particular change, or what would have happened anyway – the trickle-up effect of changes in the legal profession. That, at least, is now changing.

I left government disappointed with the progress I had been able to make on judicial diversity, and frustrated about the unsatisfactory situation we had created in relation to the most senior appointments. The 'solutions' in the 2005

Constitutional Reform Act to the 'problems' of insufficiently diverse appointments being made by the Lord Chancellor alone had created problems of their own. The law of unintended consequences was hard at work.

The jury is out. It is too soon to say what the impact of changes currently afoot will be. Twenty of Baroness Neuberger's fifty-three recommendations have been implemented in full, with all but a very small handful of the remainder under way, including those requiring primary legislation. The Crime and Courts Bill is making its way through Parliament.

My guess, though, would be that these changes will have an impact, both on making speedier progress towards a diverse judiciary and on securing the right balance between the executive, Parliament and the judiciary in relation to judicial appointments, but a smaller impact than I would like.

Most of this audience will probably be relieved to hear that I am not suggesting women-only shortlists for judicial appointments. But I do say that the system has got to try a lot harder, and that means leadership from the very top. Canada has done it. The United States is doing it. We are the international backmarkers on judicial diversity and that is not a good place to be.

And I also just offer you this gypsy's warning. As with other areas of public life, such as with women bishops, in the absence of concerted action and clear progress, there could come a moment when the failure – and it is a failure – to promote people other than the standard white male barristers to the judiciary becomes a matter of much wider public attention.

advocacy, quality of, 23
AF (No. 3), 40
Al-Khawaja judgment, 31, 40
Al-Skeini judgment, 33
Alconbury judgment, 33, 35
asylum seekers, rights of, 37–8
Auld Review, 16
Auld, Sir Robin, 16

Bar Professional Training Course,
    73
Bennett, Catherine, 15
Bingham, Lord Chief Justice Lord,
    19, 33, 35, 43
Birmingham Six, 14
Blair, Tony, 9, 27
Blunkett, David, 18, 20
Bratza, Sir Nicolas, 40, 49
Brown, Lord, 33
Brown v. *Stort*, 43
Butler-Sloss, Elizabeth, 65

Cafcass, 22
Callaghan, James, 8
Cameron, David, 69
Canada, judicial appointments
    in, 77
CCTV, 10
Chahal v. *UK*, 30, 47
choice of court, 14

Church of England, women bishops
    in, 51, 77
Civil Service, diversity in, 70
Clarke, Kenneth, 59
Clinton, Bill, 61
Collins, Lawrence, 65
constitutional amendments, 46
Constitutional Reform Act 2005,
    52, 57, 59, 72
  aims of, 53
  responsibilities of the Lord
    Chancellor, 53, 56, 76
Cook, Robin, 28
corruption, noble cause, 6
Council of Ministers (Council of
    the European Union),
    32, 45
  qualified majority voting, 45
courts
  defence of individuals against
    arbitrary or oppressive power
    of the state, 37
  efficiency and effectiveness
    of, 54
  powers of Supreme Court, 46
  understanding of the cultural and
    political norms within which
    they operate, 38
crime, 3
  changing trends in, 3

effect of the technological revolution on prevention and investigation of crime, 10

number committed and number brought to trial, 18

unreported, unrecorded and uninvestigated, 4

Crime and Courts Bill, 55–6, 59, 76–7

tipping point provisions, 72

Crime and Disorder Act, 20

criminal courts, future of, 1–22

Criminal Justice Act 2003, 17–18, 21

criminal justice system

changes to, 8

defendants' choice of court, 14, 16

effect of the technological revolution on prevention and investigation of crime, 10

efficiency and effectiveness of, 16, 24

focus on needs of victims, 24

integrity of, 24

professionalism of, 24

public confidence in, 5

regional autonomy, 22

resistance to reform, 9

role of juries, 12

scandals, 8

sentencing guidelines, 20

structure of, 2

Criminal Law Act 1977, 8

Crown court, 17

Crown Prosecution Service, 8, 21

Davis, David, 41, 43

democracy, 12, 37

democratic mandate, 41

democratic override, 26, 45–6

discrimination, positive, 66, 68–71

diversity

advantages of, 61, 63, 72

advocacy, 66–7

'business case' for, 61

in the judiciary, 60–77

and merit, 67, 71

progress in improving the judiciary, 63–4

statistics and evaluation of, 76

DNA matching technology, 10, 40, 44

Dobbs, Linda, 65

Dred Scott v. *Sandford*, 46

employment, 4

Endicott, Timothy, 47

Equal Opportunities Commission, 68

equality, 61

of ethnicity, 51

of gender, 51, 68

of income, 62

and opportunity, 62

ethnic minorities in the judiciary, 63–4, 66

European Commission on Human Rights, 32

European Convention on Human Rights, 7, 29

incorporation into UK law, 28, 33

interpretation by British courts, 32, 36

European Convention on Human Rights (cont.)
    interpretations of, 25
    a 'living instrument', 41–2
European Court of Human Rights, 30, 45
    directives, 45
    enforcement mechanisms, 45
European Court of Justice, 26
European Union
    Constitution, 42
    parliaments of member states, 26
    UK referendum on membership, 42

fairness, 61, 63
Falconer, Baron Charles, 72
financial sector
    fraud in, 18
    regulation of, 18
forensic techniques, 10
fraud, 18
    difficulties of bring cases to trial, 18
    serious cases heard by special tribunals, 17
Fraud Trials Committee, 17
Freedom of Information Act, 27

gangs, immunity from police, 6
Gardner, Edward, 28
Genn, Hazel, 71
Grayling, Chris, 59
Grieve, Dominic, 48

Hale, Baroness, 25, 34, 40, 65
    mirror principle, 34–5

Hazell, Robert, 28
Heads of Division of the Court of Appeal, appointment of, 56
High Court, judicial appointments, 52
Hirst judgment, 31, 40
HM Courts and Tribunal Service, 20
Hoffmann, Lord, 43, 47
homosexuality, 63
Howard, Michael, 47
human rights, 7
    culture of, 11
    determination of what constitutes human rights, 42
    protection of, 43
    in the United Kingdom, 50
Human Rights Act, 10, 13
    agreement on, 29
    aims of, 44
    controversial nature of, 29
    declarations of incompatibility, 38
    and Europe, 25–50
    and the European Convention on Human Rights, 29, 31
    interpretation by British courts, 27
    Liberal Democrat/Labour working party, 28
    mirror principle, 33
    preparation and implementation of, 27
    requirement to 'take into account' four categories of texts, 31, 33

section 1, 31
section 2, 31, 33, 36
section 4, 38, 56
section 12, 39
statements of compatibility, 38
success of, 11, 25

International Summit on Judicial
    Diversity, 75
Irvine of Lairg, Lord, 25, 31–2,
    43, 49

James Committee, 2
Judge, Lord, 34
judge-only trials, 13, 17
    arguments for, 18
judges
    power of, 60
    qualifications and experience
        required, 60
    removal from office, 52
Judges' Rules, 7
judicial appointments, 51–74
    appearance of fairness in, 53
    'caring effect', 65
    and diversity, 54
    diversity as a criterion for, 67
    encouragement of people to
        apply to become judges, 74
    of ethnic minority candidates, 66
    fairness and transparency in, 75
    feedback to candidates who are
        not appointed, 75
    'pat on the back' approach, 75
    'prestige effect' in the difference
        between senior and lower level
        appointments, 65

reform of the system, 53
selection bias, 71
'solely on merit', 71–2
statistics and evaluation of, 76
Judicial Appointments
    Commission, 54, 64, 75
    responsibilities of, 54
    selection panels, 54, 72
    and the 'tap on the shoulder'
        approach, 75
judicial continuity, 21
judiciary
    connection between the senior
        judiciary and the executive, 57
    diversity in, 60–77
    independence of, 19, 52–3
    and the Lord Chancellor, 58
    and the political class, 39
    public confidence in, 52
    quality of, 7, 30
    quality of decisions, 52
    a reflection of the society it
        serves, 60
    relationship with Parliament,
        19
    resistance to intervention in the
        running of courts, 19
    terms and conditions, 76
    under-representation of women,
        ethnic minority judges, gay
        and lesbian judges and
        disabled judges in, 61, 65
juries
    and either-way cases, 13
    and fraud trials, 13, 17
    jury nobbling, 13
    role of, 12

justice, 61, 63
Justice Select Committee, 19–20

Kennedy of the Shaws, Baroness
    (Helena Kennedy), 12
Klug, Francesca, 28
Kray gang, 6

Labour Party
    ethnic minority MPs, 69
    shortlists of women in selection
        of candidates, 68
    women MPs, 69
law
    consistency and predictability, 36
    uncertainty about, 36
    values of, 61
law and order as a political issue, 5
Lawrence, Stephen, 10, 62
legal aid rules, 16
legal profession
    diversity in, 73
    expansion in numbers of lawyers
        in training, 73
    and family responsibilities, 74
    proportion of women silks, 74
    retention and promotion in, 73
    role in encouraging people to
        apply for judicial
        appointments, 73
Legal Week, Big Question survey, 74
Leveson, Sir Brian, 51
Limbuela judgment, 37–8
Local Government Act 1988, 63
Lord Chancellor
    discretion of, 58
    and the judiciary, 58

lower-level judicial
    appointments, 55
responsibility for judicial
    appointments, 52–4, 58–9
senior judicial appointments,
    55–6
Lord Chief Justice
    appointment of, 54
    responsibility for judicial
        appointments, 55

Maclennan, Robert, 28
Mackay of Clashfern, Lord, 65
Macpherson, Sir William, 62
magistrates' courts, reform of, 15
margin of appreciation, 26, 44
Marper judgment, 31, 40, 44
Marriott, Arthur, 65
Maxwell Confait case, 8
McCann v. *UK*, 30
members of parliament
    ethnic minority, 69
    maternity and paternity leave, 70
    women, 69
merit, and diversity, 67, 71
ministerial accountability, 22
mirror principle, 33, 35
Mode of Trial Bill, 9, 15, 17
Mohamed, R v. *Secretary of State for
    Foreign & Commonwealth
    Affairs*, 39
moral panics, 3
Morsi, Mohamed, 51

ne bis in idem rule, 10
Neuberger, Baroness, 73, 75–7
Neuberger, Lord, 67, 73

Parliament
  gender composition of, 68
  respect for, 39
  role in the Sentencing Council, 20
Parliament Acts, 15, 63
parliamentary sovereignty, 11, 28,
  36–7, 57
Philips Royal Commission, 8, 14, 22
Pinnock judgment, 33
Police and Criminal Evidence Act
  1984, 7–8
police service, 2, 5
  city and borough forces, 2
  complaints against, 6
  corruption in, 5
  ethnic minority officers in, 63
  and gangs, 6
  leadership of, 6
  police discipline cases, 10
  regulation of powers of arrest and
    detention of suspects, 7, 11
  variation of prosecution
    arrangements from force to
    force, 21
political class, and the judiciary, 39
power, 42
'prestige effect', 65
Prevention of Crime Act 1953, 3
prison population, 4
prisoner voting rights, 27, 40, 47
prisons, 'payment by results'
  schemes, 21
privacy, development of the law
  of, 39
Proceeds of Crime Act 2002, 19
Prosecution of Offenders Act
  1985, 8

prosecutions, resources for
  prosecutors, 23
prosecutions, variation of
  arrangements for, 21

Quality Assurance Scheme for
  Advocates, 23

R v. *Davis*, 39
R v. *Twomey*, 13
ratio decidendi, 35–6
regional autonomy, 22
Regulation of Investigatory Powers
  Act 2000, 11
Richardson gang, 6
Rodger, Lord, 40, 45
Roskill Committee, 17
Royal Commission on Criminal
  Justice, 14
Royal Commission on Criminal
  Procedure, 8, 21
rule of law, 12, 49
Runciman, Viscount, 14–16

Sales, Sir Philip, 33, 36
Scoppola v. *Italy (No. 3)*, 48
Sealy, Ruth, 70
Second World War, 1
Senior President of Tribunals,
  responsibility for judicial
  appointments, 55
sentencing
  guidelines for, 20
  predictability in, 21
Sentencing Guidelines Council,
  20
separation of powers, 30

Sex Discrimination (Election
    Candidates) Act 2002, 69
sovereignty, 42
stare decisis, 35–6
Starmer, Keir, 11, 21, 23
Strasbourg Court (European Court
    of Human Rights), 26
  and British institutions, 40
  and British politicians, 41
  case law, 35
  conflict with the UK parliament,
    27
  determination of human rights,
    42, 45
  expansion of its jurisdiction, 26,
    35, 41–2, 49
  judgments and advisory
    opinions, 31
  lack of democratic override, 26,
    48
  margin of appreciation, 26, 44
  Scoppola v. *Italy (No. 3)*, 48
  as a Supreme Court of Europe,
    26, 41
Straw, Jack, *Last Man Standing:*
    Memoirs of a Political
    Survivor, 62
Sumption, Justice Jonathan, 43,
    66–7, 72
Supreme Courts, powers of, 46

Taylor, Lord, 64
technological revolution in the
    prevention and investigation
    of crime, 10

call data, 10
CCTV, 10
DNA matching technology,
    10
television, and perceptions of
    crime, 5
Thatcher, Margaret, 68
Todd, Michael, 73

UK Supreme Court, 54
  appointments to, 56, 59
  discretion under the Human
    Rights Act, 57
  and the European Convention
    on Human Rights, 56
Ullah judgment, 33, 35
United States
  Constitution, 46
  judicial appointments in, 77
  Supreme Court, 46

Vinnicombe, Susan, 70

'Ways and Means Act', 6
women
  'caring effect' in judicial
    appointments, 65
  in the judiciary, 64
  quality of MPs, 69
  quotas for in business,
    70
  under-representation in the
    judiciary, 61

Zander, Michael, 14